Publisher: Blueshield Publishers

ISBN: 978-978-991-237-7

Email: blueshieldpublishers@gmail.com

Phone :08161516628

Print @ Newman Int'l Press: +234 803 531 8936

CONTENTS

FOREWORD

It gives me great delight to write the Foreword to this evocatively titled book, *Tomorrow's Leaders*. The book's forte is the depth of treatment by the author and the topicality of its subject matter. Leadership deficit is widely acknowledged as a major impediment to Nigeria's wholesome development. This is why this book is so timely and particularly valuable for its well informed and incisive intervention in the discourse on governance, leadership and development in Nigeria and Africa. The author, Pastor Andrew Umoru, has brought his decades of private sector engagement and service in pastoral ministry to bear on his handling of the subject matter of leadership in the Nigerian and comparative contexts. It is evident that he himself exemplifies and applies the principles that he has so lucidly enunciated in this book. Key issues analyzed in the six main chapters of the book include aspects of leadership, including qualification, recruitment, succession, vision, and innovation, as well as culture, diversity, change management, business ethics, organizational theory and practice, and fraud management. This book is a compelling narrative informed by current secondary literature and pithy quotes from leaders across generations and nations.

Altogether, *Tomorrow's Leaders,* is a harvest of the author's ideas, practical experience and deep insights into the human condition. The book is highly recommended to the general reader, as well as mentors, counsellors and aspiring leaders. It is a valuable resource that will enrich institutions, individual lives and ministries.

Ayodeji Olukoju, Ph.D., FNAL

Distinguished Professor, University of Lagos June 2018

ENDORSEMENTS

"A profound resource with fresh insights that shape our perspectives on leadership. This book makes a compelling reading and provides tools for raising and equipping transformational leaders and change agents."

Professor Tunde Opeibi, PhD

(Professor of English- Digital Cultures & Discourse Studies Univ. of Lagos)

Life Fellow, Alexander von Humboldt Foundation, Germany

Member, Executive Board, Global Outlook for Digital Humanities (GO::DH)

Founding Chair, Digital Humanities Research Unit, University of Lagos

President, Digital Humanities Association of Nigeria (DHAN)

https://www.iash.ed.ac.uk/current-fellows

www.dhunilag.com

“There is no doubt that the failure in leadership should account for eighty percent of our problems in Africa.

Our political leaders (rather rulers) would prefer to die in office than make room for younger blood. Unfortunately, the younger ones appear not to have learned much as the author noted "leaders find it easy to align with the position of the older politicians "and will probably just continue where the oldies have left off if given a chance.

The civil service mentality, instead of changing is now spilling over to the private sector. Though they complain, but still continue with the practice paying ghost workers, not minding the lack of productivity. Until we have more youths taking the future in their hands and taking a leap forward, Africa will continue to be backward.

We know that Africans are equally gifted and intelligent, this has been proven and over as they excel in the western world - where the environment is conducive. So, what is wrong with Africa? The reader will garner more than sufficient reasons and explanations from this book. I have read only the first two chapters; but I have no doubt of the likely impact of the whole book- I just wish it is not read as an academic exercise and added to the library.

The book is written in a very readable and enjoyable prose but unfortunately, one cannot but sigh very deeply at our plight. Who will deliver Africa? What is the future of our young ones? I do hope that the complete book gives ideas that can be taken up to answer some of the questions. Happy reading."

M. O. Onasanya (Mrs) FCCA. FCA

Mrs. Moronkeji Onasanya is a Chartered Accountant with close to fifty years of professional experience in the private sector locally and internationally. A former staffer with Gestetner Ltd, London, Mrs. Onasanya spent most of her career years with UAC Group where she retired as Head of Finance, and Executive Director. She was thereafter appointed to the board of Skye Bank Plc where she served as Vice Chairman and Chairman at various times. She has also served on boards and governing councils of higher institutions, blue chip companies and professional associations.

ACKNOWLEDGMENT

It would be very necessary to mention a few from the long list of helpers and volunteers who contributed immensely and invaluably to the conclusion of this work.

My loving wife, Glory, was there all the time providing and creating an enabling environment during the years it took to conceptualize and gather materials for this project. And my dearest friend and confidant, Pastor Gordian I. Nweke, and his precious family in Ontario, Canada, who mobilized and took charge of the printing aspect. Dr. Ayo Oluwaguna graciously provided the concept for the cover page, while Pastor Abiodun Odo helped in the initial arrangement. I cannot but mention my dear brother, and distinguished Professor of History and Strategic Studies, Professor Ayodeji Olukoju, who proof read the book and wrote a very beautiful foreword to it. Sister Onyinye Okoh did the final reading. Others worth mentioning here are my dear friends, Pastor Segun Babatope, Pastor Emeka Izeze, Professor Tunde Opeibi and our beloved mother,

Mrs M.O. Onasanya. Together with my distinguished Professors at AIU, Honolulu, USA.

DEDICATION

This book is dedicated to God Almighty, for His mercies and grace.

REVIEW OF TOMORROW'S LEADERS

Every organization flies or falls, depending on the quality of its leadership. The buck indeed stops on the desk of the leader. If there is therefore, an overarching need in the society today, it is to find a full-orbed leadership material. This is a historic search that will continue so long as new talent and creativity are needed to lift the well-being of the human community. I see this book as a continuation of that search. Its strength is in targeting the young. *Tomorrow's Leaders* should therefore, be seen as an inspiration to the young to recognize their role in history and face the challenge with confidence, creativity and competence. There are more than enough nuggets in this book to help that endeavor. In the end, putting the wisdom and knowledge packed into this book is one way to make the future better than today.

Emeka Izeze

Former Managing Director/Editor-in-Chief of Guardian Newspapers Limited, Lagos.

CHAPTER ONE

WHO IS A LEADER?

"Leadership is the art of getting someone else to do something you want done because he wants to do it".

- Dwight O. Eisenhower

People are focusing on the subject of leadership today more than ever before. From the local village setting to the busy capital cities of our world, the importance of leadership cannot be over- emphasized. And from the small and medium enterprises (SME) to the multinational companies and big conglomerates, leadership has taken the centre stage.

Leaders are needed in our world today more than ever before to provide direction and drive the nation or the organization to greater heights. Success is not achieved because of the availability of resources, be it human, financial or material, but the availability of leaders to harness these factors to achieve set objectives. Leaders are involved in strategic and critical thinking to bring about results in a fast- competitive world. The question is, who is a leader?

At the very basic level, a leader is someone who leads others. But what is it that makes someone a leader? And what is it about you that attracts people to you and make them want to follow you? And what is it about being a leader that some people have so much mastered and used to their advantage? What can you then do to be a leader?

Let us start by examining how leadership has been defined. Dr. Paul Hersey, who developed the situational leadership model in the late 1960s, defined leadership as "working with and through others to achieve objectives". From this definition, anyone in a position whose achievement depends upon the support of others is playing the role of a leader. He or she is a person who has a vision, and a commitment, skill and drive to achieve that vision, but requires others who can work with him or her to fulfill the ultimate objective. Powerful ideas most likely originate from individuals who will then need to share the ideas with others. He or she will require the input of others who will help bring the vision to a reality. A tree, it is said, cannot make a forest. Every leader requires others working and contributing to bring about the fulfillment of the vision received.

Leadership is further defined as "the process in which an individual influences the group of individuals to attain a common goal." A leader may possess many qualities, yet the ability to influence stands out. Influence is the key to getting people do what is needed to arrive at organizational objectives. The ability to command followership is the key quality that aspiring leaders must possess.

Many leaders have come up on the African political scene, but none, has been able to generate the kind of global influence like the iconic Nelson Mandela of South Africa. He was one of the most influential persons in the twenty-first century. His legendary influence cuts across countries and continents, and many saw him as a model. There are other great leaders who have made a significant mark in our world; Mahatma Gandhi, Martin Luther King, Winston Churchill, George Washington and Abraham Lincoln, to mention but a few. Influence, however, does not grow on trees; it is something that must be carefully cultivated and developed before it begin to blossom. Some leaders are popular because of the solutions they generate to our everyday lives. Albert Einstein, Thomas Edison, Bill Gates, Steve Jobs and others in this category improved our standard of living, invented machines and methods that simplified the process of carrying out our everyday tasks. Others unfortunately, are popular because of the problems they created. Adolf Hitler and ldi-Amin of Uganda are in that rank. Confirming the fact that influence can either be on the positive side, bringing about solutions to human needs, or on the negative side, complicating issues and adding to existing problems. These leaders of influence, whether on the positive or negative side possess the ability to change people and sway them to a different direction.

Adolf Hitler was a master in that regard. His speeches had such a mesmerizing effect on the ordinary Germans that within a few years, he was able to lead Germany down the abyss of self- destruction, The Nazi party he created and led, ran the concentration camps, the factories of death in Auschwitz, Treblinka and other places where millions of innocent Jews and others classified as deplorables were unfortunately gassed to death.

A leader of influence should possess many attributes including a good character, honesty, trustworthiness and faithfulness. Other attributes include, creativity, confidence, ability to inspire, a positive attitude and willingness to train successors. This is of utmost importance because success without successors is failure. John Quincy Adams once said: "If your actions inspire others to dream more, learn more, do more and become more, you are a leader." Our leadership must benefit others and produce results. To be successful in leadership, a leader must showcase many skills and abilities. As Ralph

Waldo Emerson stated, "Do not follow where the path may lead. Go instead where there is no path and leave a trail." It's like going to where the opportunity will be rather than staying where it is right now. "The best way to predict the future is to create it" This quote is credited to two great people; Abraham Lincoln and Peter Drucker, both known for their proven ability in leadership.

So, leaders take us to new, untested destinations, they seems not to be satisfied with just having to wait for the future, they create the future themselves and take the prize by the force of their imagination. This kind of inventiveness is a very important quality in leadership, as those who are considered great leaders, are such as had a vision at the beginning, and persuaded others to follow.

To add to the attributes and skills already outlined, a leader must possess skills such as the ability to make decisions, solve problems and think strategically. They must equally possess the ability to manage change, build teams and deliver on targets. This is what makes the ubject of organizational leadership very essential and entral to those who aspire to be leaders or who desire to be better leaders.

DEVELOPING TOMORROW'S LEADERS

Life changes so fast; it's like a fast-moving train that one needs to catch up with or be left behind. New ideas are generated to replace the old ones. Everyone who aspires to be relevant in whatever field of human endeavor must be willing to improve and update or become obsolete. Once we run out of ideas, we are benched, and set aside; and passed over to give room to new emerging leaders with better ideas. If you are not current, then you cannot be correct. In developing the future leaders, the following critical success areas are to be considered:

A. Ideas in Leadership

Leaders generate winning ideas. But where do good ideas come from? There are obviously as many answers as there are authors on this subject. Ideas, they say, rule the world Putting those ideas to work has improved our quality of life. Probably the most important scientific discovery during the 20th century was Einstein's theory of relativity. But we need to understand how new ideas, such as Einstein's theory, come about. Einstein built upon and improved the work and knowledge of the centuries of men and women that had come before him. Galileo did the same when he built his popular theories upon the work performed by Copernicus, Kepler and Brahe. What are we learning here? Do not overlook work already done; that is a good ground to start. Thereafter, improvements and additions would be made.

It is very true that we utilize the efforts of other people to form new and better ideas. T.S. Eliot summed this up when he stated, "good writers borrow. Great writers steal." Perhaps the Internet with its vast information store is allowing us to be even more efficient thieves!

Yet many others came across their wonderful ideas just by taking a stroll into the wooded areas and suburbs of their countryside homes, sitting by the riverbank or all alone in a quiet garden. Some great writers have the structure or sketch of their work stream down into their minds as they watch nature, they will then go ahead to represent these in black and white and become a success.

I know of a popular writer in Nigeria that is said to receive his inspiration while meditating on the grounds of his country home. To the extent that visitors who visit during those times are said to have visited 'when he was not at home' yes he was, so to speak, but away receiving an idea whose flow should not be disturbed or interrupted by visitors. That leader is Prof. Wole Soyinka, who won the nation's only Nobel Prize for Literature in1986.

For further reading about how leaders generate their ideas, one can rely on a good number of materials found in many well researched books by authors who wrote on this subject. A detailed analysis of the book "Where Good Ideas

Come From: The Natural History of Innovation" by Steven Johnson comes handy; with John Locke's "An Essay Concerning Human Understanding" published in 1690, which gave the world a truly different theory regarding the formation of knowledge, providing a very useful guide.

Leadership is not an activity that is mysterious. Avolio (2005) points out that leadership is not a mysterious activity and, therefore, the ability to perform complex tasks is widely distributed to people. Some people believe that leaders are born to lead and yet made by some mysterious confluence of events and chance. What some may refer to as the hand of providence, favour or good luck.

B. Vision in Leadership

Leaders see afar; they see far enough to distinguish themselves from the rest of the people who are myopic. Leaders see a problem that needs to be solved, an opportunity that needs to be seized, or a goal that needs to be achieved. It may be a subject that no one wants to study or even consider; or simply something that no one else is interested in. Whatever it is that the leader chooses to be the subject of his attention, he attacks it with a single-minded effort and determination.

Whether the goal may be: to double the company's annual sales, develop a new product that will address or provide a solution to a certain problem, or start a company that can make an immediate impact, the leader always must have a clear vision and target in mind. This is the big picture that only leaders can see. Thomas Edison saw the need to invent the light bulb and went all out for it. Many of the best technology companies in the Silicon Valley today started on a small scale, some in a small garage but they retained the vision for a world-wide impact. But what has been achieved already is certainly not the end; for even the giant computer software companies in California are unsure what a little high school graduate sitting in his father's basement or garage may come up with in a couple of days. By the end of World War II information was doubling every twenty-five years, but right now, information doubles every twelve months. And who knows what the future holds?

C. Leadership Drive

Thomas Edison was said to have tried and failed more than a hundred times, but he was determined to see his vision through, and that was critical to his success at last in finding the right filament for the light bulb. It is not enough to have an idea or a vision. Lots of people possess excellent vision only to fail at the point of implementation. A great percentage of new businesses and ideas fail due to lack of determination and drive to see the vision through.

Determination is a passion for the idea, an inner motivation or drive, or some sense of commitment to see your vision through. Whatever or however it may be viewed, it is the strength within that lets leaders move their vision forward in spite of present or perceived obstacles, despite the multitude of people saying, "it can't e done", "it's too late, too costly", "we tried it before and it ailed" or a dozen other excuses and problems that may lot the horizon. The leader with determination perseveres and forges ahead. It's like the biblical story of Jacob, who said, 'I will not let you go except you bless me". The determination and desperation combine to deliver the results and make the dream to be realized.

There are traits that set leaders apart and make them different from other people. Some people are born with these traits and characteristics, yet many others develop them as they improve their lives generally and their leadership abilities specifically. These are not magic wands. They are things that can be done and have been done through leaning and self-improvement and development.

IMPORTANCE OF LEADERS – AFRICA'S CASE STUDY

The importance of leaders in our world today cannot be over emphasized. Poor leadership is the main reason some countries are underdeveloped and very poor in terms of productivity, growth and human development. Corruption, mismanagement and bad leadership are the biggest problems in Africa right now. This is the root cause of poverty and underdevelopment in the continent as a whole.

One cannot fully understand Africa until one has spent considerable time there. One can be misled to think that Africa is a 'dark continent' a jungle where nothing works; and if one rely on stories as told by some early explorers and writers who briefly visited Africa and sat down to write the story as they imagined it, one will miss the true picture. Their stories and accounts are often tainted by the influences of contemporary prejudice and xenophobia. Reading through books like the *Heart of Darkness* by Joseph Conrad based on his brief voyage through the Congo

River; one will go with a completely biased image of Africa. Professor Chinua Achebe, the popular African author and veteran storyteller from Eastern Nigeria described Conrad's work as 'a story in which the very humanity of black people is called in question.' (An Image of Africa, and the Problem with Nigeria, 1983: 16).

Sitting down under the moon light in the northern part of Edo State where I spent my early years, the African story is a sweet one. From the oral tradition passed on by our forefathers, our people were brought up to respect elders, work hard in their farms and maintain good neighborliness. Up till this very moment, there are huge unbelievable economic opportunities in Nigeria and many parts of sub-Sahara Africa. It has, during the industrial revolution supplied the world with cheap raw materials which powered the economy of Europe at that time. The problem really with Africa is leadership. Chief Emeka Odumegwu Ojukwu, the military leader who precipitated the Nigerian civil war which lasted between July 6, 1967, and January 15, 1970, described Chief Obafemi Awolowo, a Nigerian nationalist, as 'the best president Nigeria never had.' How true that is. Africa's best, for one reason or the other are either unable or unwilling to participate in the leadership of their nations for many reasons. Some are unable to cope with the violence and ruthlessness that characterize the electoral processes in their countries - which some has christened the do-or-die politics or garrison politics.

Nelson Mandela led South Africa as president for just a single term in office. Rising African leaders of Nigerian extraction in the likes of Professor Wole Soyinka, a Nobel Laureate for literature, the late Professor Chinua Achebe and the former Secretary General of the Commonwealth of Nations, Chief Emeka Anyaoku, have all not fully participated in the politics of Nigeria, perhaps because its exclusive and dangerous. In a country where some are ready to kill to maintain their place in office, there is little room for those who are not as desperate.

Nigeria is Africa's largest producer of crude oil with a maximum production capacity of 2.5 million barrels per day. Since the nation's independence in 1960, more than $380 billion has been stolen or wasted by the nation's leaders. Some estimates have over $500 billion wasted through corruption, nepotism, over- invoicing, contract inflation and embezzlement.

Leadership development is perhaps more important to the African continent than anywhere else in the world today. Travelling through some of the poorest countries in Africa, like the Central African Republic (CAR), Burundi, Somalia, Sierra Leon, Chad and Niger Republic, Sudan and many others, one immediately comes to the ominous conclusion that except something is done very quickly about leadership in Africa, the future of the continent may remain bleak.

In Nigeria, for instance, where we pride ourselves about having put in place democratic governance, the dividends of democracy circulate only among a select few. This is like a scene from George Orwell's *Animal Farm* where all animals were said to be equal 'but some animals were more equal than the others'.

There is need to shift our focus from our present fire-fighting approach to developing the next generation of leaders to take over the baton if we expect a future turn around. We must desist from the practice of recycling leaders in office when we know fully well that they are too old, and with the same old archaic ideas that had stagnated the economy and blocked progress.

Unfortunately, many of these upcoming leaders find it easy to align with the position of the older politicians whose ideas have brought the various countries into the situation they find themselves today. We cannot expect better results if we continue with business as usual. The vast human and material resources and opportunities in the continent require effective leadership to manage into the success we all desire. With good leadership, Africa can ise beyond imagination and join the comity of nations egarded as economic superpowers today.

Decades after the achievement of independence from her colonial masters, Africa is still home to majority of the world's poorest countries despite the abundant human and material resources. A continent that has the most endowed and fertile lands of our world and the richest continent on earth in terms of natural resources has become so damaged through bad leadership that the world is wondering what's going on there. This, to me, is the most serious problem the continent faces.

Based on research, Africa's economy, is still very weak compared to other developing economies in Asia and Latin America. It remains abysmally weak, and accounts for less than 1.2 percent of the World's GDP (World Bank, 2006), even though more than 10 per cent of the world's population live there. (UNDP,1996).

Africa has around six hundred million hectares of uncultivated arable land, which is roughly sixty per cent of the global total. Yet farming is still mainly undertaken through the means of outdated technology and technique which results in low productivity. African cereal yields, for example, are just over one-third of the developing world average and have barely increased in thirty years. One major challenge is that as much as eighty per cent of Africa's agriculture still depends on rainfall rather than irrigation. (Fareed Zakaria, GPS, November 6th, 2012). Africa will be unable to compete with other continents in the area of food production if she continues to practice subsistence farming. What Africa need right now is charismatic, conscientious and visionary, young and agile leadership to connect the dots and bring about development in every sector. Leadership is, and has continued to be the problem.

I have often listened to people who put the blame of African under-development squarely on the shoulders of her colonial masters who helped drain the continent of her raw materials, together with her best brains to power the industrial revolution of the eighteen century in Europe and America. While I sincerely believe that the countries that were involved in such brutal repression and exploitation of Africa continent still owe us, not just a verbal apology but some kind of reparation or restitution; it is obvious that Africa has come a long way since after regaining her independence to advance and move forward. It is now time for Africa to move forward after these many years of self-rule.

From the middle part of the 20th century, there was a strong prospect both within and outside the continent of Africa that the future will be better and more prosperous because of the much-cherished freedom and the joy of seeing African leaders assuming office to lead African people. However, that hope never stood the test of time. Many African leaders were discovered not to be the true nationalists they portrayed themselves to be. There was cluelessness and self-perpetuation; selfishness coupled with massive looting of the nation's treasuries. It is in

Africa you find leaders who refuse to step down when their tenure expires. They prefer to die in office rather than hand over power to on-coming leaders. Although the African Union has in recent times refused in a number of instances to recognize leaders who fail to respect the will of the people after democratic elections, they still must come together and see how to pressure the remaining sit-tight heads of governments to call it quit and create room for a fresh start.

CHAPTER TWO

LEADERSHIP AND GROWTH

"We cannot solve our problems with the same level of thinking that created them"

- Albert Einstein.

Albert Einstein observed that the problems we face today cannot be solved on the same level of thinking we were when we created them. Under the current business climate, you either innovate or you are isolated. Corporate organizations all over the world are presently occupied by a new enthusiasm for rapid innovation and growth. The opportunities are just increasing; with fast-paced technologies, rapid global expansion, changing business models, mergers and acquisitions happening everywhere from America to China, from India to Indonesia. In order to benefit from these opportunities, corporate leaders are confronting a new set of challenges - the need for better leaders with talents. These leaders must possess vision and should have the ability to point that future out to their followers. 'Good thinking produces more good thinking if you make it a habit' (Maxwell, 2005:12). How true this is today! Leaders must lead with vision in order to inspire followership.

In business, as well as in every field of human endeavor, even in church or sports administration there is a clear need for leaders who can think fast and operate globally - and those require far more than knowing how to set up a firm, run for elections or start a Non-Governmental Organization.

To achieve success, today's leaders must be able to lead with their heads (that is manage complexity), with their hearts (manage diversity) and with their guts (which is about managing uncertainty). A truly effective and efficient global leader has high capacity, can articulate a point of view, formulate winning strategies, lead global teams and lead the change. We need also to understand that to develop effective global leaders is a matter of competitive advantage. This is an investment worth making because it secures the future of the organization and brings relief and satisfaction at the end. This, perhaps, is what Africa desperately needs.

Looking at our world today, one can see vividly the importance and impact of effective leadership. It is important to note that young leaders have emerged to fill the vacancies previously reserved for old men and women, especially in Europe and America. A lot of young leaders have emerged in politics and business. Leadership is very important because it provides an inspirational figure to lead other groups of people towards greater accomplishments. Leadership provides the foundation for solid ideas and excellence, showing others that anything is, and can be, possible. Leaders move to where the opportunity will be, not where it is right now.

With good leadership, corporate culture is not a forced idea, but it is developed and embraced. The vision and goal is communicated and employees feel that they are an important part of the business and they are motivated to contribute to the growth of the organization.

LEADERSHIP STYLES

A. AUTHORITATIVE STYLE

Douglas McGregor created and developed theory X and Y which is about human motivation. Theory X presupposes that people are inherently and perpetually lazy and will avoid work if possible. Because people will avoid responsibility, they will need to be directed, controlled and coerced with punishment in order to get them to produce and meet organizational goals and objectives. The theory equally assumes that people want to be directed and controlled since they lack any ambition in themselves to stimulate achievement and are only concerned about job security.

Some managers adopt this theory and are therefore autocratic and authoritative in their management style.

Leaders who adopt this style are in the habit of not accepting inputs from subordinates. They tell their employees what they want done and how they want it done, without asking for advice from their followers. This style adopts know-it-all approach, yelling on subordinates and using demeaning language; it encapsulates leading by threats and intimidation.

Reading through the national bestseller book titled: *The 48 Laws of Power* by Robert Greene (Penguin Books, 2000) provides insights into this style of leadership. Law 2 is about concealing your intentions and never revealing your intentions. While Law 4 is to always say less than necessary. Law 5 is about crushing your enemy totally. Leaders who read materials like these are often very autocratic in leadership. They are mostly power drunk and lead with harshness. This style of leadership should only be used on rare occasions especially if you want to gain more commitment from your staff but bossing people around has no place in today's world.

When leaders imbibe this style of leadership, everything is regimented. It is like a military barracks where the General Officer Commanding (GOC) holds sway. Everything is done by shouting out commands with the corresponding response - '"YES SIR". I heard of the funny story of an NCO (Non-Commissioned Officer) Private Stephen (not real name) who applied for his annual leave which was approved during one of the mandatory early morning exercises/briefings. The commanding officer shouted: "PRIVATE STEPHEN!" who then stepped forward, falling out of the line with a salute "SIR". The GOC then shouted the approval to him at the top of his voice this way: "YOU'RE WARNED TO PROCEED ON YOUR ANNUAL LEAVE TOMORROW!" "THANKS SIR" came the response from Private Stephen. Leaders who use this approach may succeed in instilling fear but will soon discover that not much can be achieved under an atmosphere of fear, intimidation and warnings. When leaders become so autocratic with too much power vested in them, they end up surrounding themselves with sycophants who are fighting for his favours and will mostly be devoid of any incentive to think for themselves or the organization; they simply follow orders.

B. PARTICIPATIVE/DEMOCRATIC STYLE

McGregor's theory Y is the opposite of theory X. This theory assumes that every man or woman has something to contribute, and that work is as natural to man as play and rest. That people are not lazy and will exercise self-direction and initiative if a conducive environment is created. It equally has the assumption that people have potential, are interested in taking on more responsibility, are creative and will work better if the pay and reward is adequate and acceptable.

The democratic style involves the leader working with one or more employees in the decision-making process. The subordinates are consulted in determining what to do and how it will be done. This is because people help build what they help create. This is the leadership style that is most successful and most acceptable to employees; it also produces the best results. However, the leader adopting this style of leadership still maintains the final decision-making authority. Using this style in leading people is not a sign of weakness; rather it is actually a sign of strength and confidence that your employees will respect.

When this style was adopted by the organization where I worked during the early '90s, it was called The New Way of Work. Staff ID cards were re-issued to highlight our first names; and we were encouraged to call each other, including even the MD, by their first names. Department Heads, which were previously like GOCs had their titles changed to Team Leaders. We were encouraged to work as a team through many briefing sessions and meetings. Stickers, T-shirts and pamphlets were distributed in a massive publicity to change our attitudes. It was called attitudinal change. All the discriminatory signs and languages like 'Junior Staff', 'Senior Staff', 'Management Staff, etc. were abolished. This new way of work proved to be effective. The company moved on to occupy the top position in the industry with production soaring, and staff motivation and satisfaction improved. This was clear evidence that greater progress comes through participatory work style than the autocratic one, because together we do it better.

When this style of leadership is adopted by a nation, it allows for freedom of expression, rule of law, freedom of the press and accommodation of different opinions. Dictators often start by silencing the press and discouraging criticisms and suppressing the opposition before imposing their authoritarian rule.

C. *DELEGATIVE/LAISSEZ FAIRE*

The leader adopting this style allows the employees to make the decisions but takes responsibility for the outcome of their actions, especially when it is positive. This is used when employees are able to plan, analyze the situation and determine what needs to be done and how to go about it. The leader does not interfere or take the lead Such leaders lead from behind.

Some argue that the boss cannot do everything; that he or she must set priorities and delegate certain tasks to others. However, it must be mentioned that delegation is different from abdication. When the Chief Executive Officer (CEO) is always away on holidays and only calls once in a blue moon to find out how things are going, it can create room for the mismanagement of the organization. Such leaders who are always away are regarded by some to be lazy. This style can only succeed when you fully trust and have complete confidence in the people below you. It must therefore be used wisely.

It should be noted that most leaders do not strictly use one style or another, but adopt whichever style that will be useful depending on the environment under which they operate.

ARE LEADERS BORN OR MADE?

Are leaders born or made? This is a very important question. Although some people are naturally more inclined to become leaders, it should be noted that their early life experience plays a very fundamental role in their future life (Mishra & Karen, 2008). In the Benin Kingdom in Nigeria, for instance, the first son of the king is designated the heir apparent. As the Crown Prince, leadership opportunity together with leadership responsibility is thrust upon him from birth. In Britain, the first born (boy or girl) of the sitting monarch is a leader from the day of birth, and may sit upon the throne as king or queen in future.

That said, it is important to point out that anybody can become a leader if only they desire and make the right efforts to do so. It is equally true that people do not have the same abilities and talents; some people are more empathetic than others, others are more energetic and yet some are more engaging than others (Mishra & Karen,

2008). This implies that every individual has his or her own unique composition of talents, dreams and motives that provide raw material for getting out the best from everyone around them (Mishra & Karen, (2008:4). Though people can be both humble and heroic, yet they are not superhuman, invulnerable or unbeatable. This means that leadership can be learned. Most of what leaders possess that enables them to lead is learned.

Leaders are not born but made. That is why leadership development is very important with regard to succession planning to secure the future of the organization. Mole (2012) has criticized conventional leadership development, highlighting the importance of contextual leadership in an essay titled 'Can Leadership be Taught?' He argued that where leadership role is defined in terms of context, it leads to increase in knowledge, change in attitude and successful performance.

REWARDS IN LEADERSHIP

Leaders are needed to steer the ship in the right direction, and they get so generously rewarded for their contributions, though many may not understand why leaders of organizations get so much pay. There has been a lot of complaints, especially in the United States, about executive pay. Many complain that the remuneration of leaders of big organizations is too large and that they normally exit the company when things fall apart, through a golden parachute.

A recent report from the Institute for Policy Studies points to a weak link between executive performance and executive pay among some of the highest-paid CEOs of American companies, and urges the United States government to push through laws that would bring CEO pay under closer scrutiny. The report titled 'Executive Excess 2013' found out that chief executives of large companies in the US received about 354 times as much pay as the average worker in America in 2012. That gap has increased since 1993, when the gap was about 195 times as much.

People often argue for equal pay for equal work, some even go to the extent of demanding uniform hourly payments across the board to all categories of staff.

Why should a CEO of a company be paid so much annually together with the huge performance bonuses they receive when their policies succeed? And why pay them those astronomical figures when leaving the organization? This has not gone down well with many staffers, especially the unskilled and semi-skilled workers at the bottom of the ladder of the organization. I remember how on several occasions the staff unions have called us out during my nearly eighteen-year career in the petroleum industry in Nigeria to protest unequal salaries and benefits. "*Monkey dey work, Baboon dey chop,*" meaning, 'we get the work done, while they get the benefits' was a very popular slogan among workers in Nigeria, especially in the '80s. We sang and danced around the company and on the streets to press home our demands and attract public attention to our plights. And where this didn't work, we embarked on strikes which have the potential of crippling the economy and/or forcing the government of the day to resign.

Frankly, CEOs spend most of their times attending to routine issues - signing documents, attending meetings and sometimes vacationing. So why do they get all that pay? The reason isn't farfetched - their strategic decisions and innovations.

STRATEGIC DECISIONS AND INNOVATIONS

The decision taken by the leadership of any organization makes or mars the organization. Of course, all the conglomerates and multinational companies will state in their corporate vision and mission statements that they plan to achieve their goals through the use of highly motivated staff - ranking the employees as their most important assets. Such goals will be thwarted if the leadership is weak.

The reason the leaders are paid so highly is not for their routine work, which any well-trained young college graduate can undertake; but for their strategic decisions about merger and acquisition, product differentiation, diversification and remodeling, sales, production and credit policies, financing and profit-sharing policies, to mention but a few.

The big conglomerates and multinational companies today require good leadership to steer them towards even greater heights and whenever the company fails to perform, the person to face the music is usually the CEO and not the general workers down the line.

The CEO of Volvo cars in North America, an organization in the struggling car manufacturing industry, John Maloney, who had held the top job since 2011 left the company in October, 2013 and Tony Nicolosi stepped in as the new CEO. Volvo's U.S. sales had slumped 7 percent that year in an expanding market and have gained little ground since the recession. The company has been squeezed by an ageing product lineup and competed poorly with other luxury brands from European, U.S. and Asian automakers.

Sports leadership (especially football) is one area in leadership where your success or failure comes out in just about ninety minutes. The head coach of a football club dictates the style of play and reads the game. He will usually receive the larger share of the blame should his team lose in a competitive match. After making a few substitutions that often lead to one or two crucial goals, he will be praised as a worthy coach whose contract should be renewed at its expiration.

Jose Mourinho, a popular coach who moved back to Chelsea Football Club in 2014 from Real Madrid is fondly referred to as '*The Special One*' because of his proven ability to turn a struggling team into a winning one. But he was kicked out from his job as Chelsea head coach in 2015 after failing to maintain the club at the top of the League table.

Manchester United FC had their worst start in 24 years under their new manager David Moyes, who succeeded legendary Alex Ferguson as Head Coach with so many silverwares to his credit. He was replaced by Louis van Gal in 2015, who was, in turn, replaced by Jose Mourinho in the 2016/17 season. The same is true in many other sports.

STRATEGIC THINKING

Almost all great leaders are great thinkers. They believe they can change the status quo; they can't wait for the future, they make the future bend to their rules. They spend much time thinking and focusing on complex problems than others until they eventually find the answers. These are the thinking leaders who help change the world. Albert Einstein falls into this category:

"It's not that I'm so smart, it's just that I stay with problems longer." - Albert Einstein.

Others are crazy enough to think differently and adopt new untested methods. They are courageous risk takers, and they end up just where their dreams ended

- in death or in life. They take the future into their hands, they have the guts, and they believe the impossible. They believe they can create a brand-new product from a brand-new idea. Steve Jobs, founder and CEO of Apple Computers, falls into this category. "The people who are crazy enough to think they can change the world are the ones who do." - Steve Jobs

When he died on October 5, 2011, at the age of 56, Steve Jobs, who was co-founder and CEO of Apple, had 241 registered patents either in his name or as co-inventor. The most successful and revolutionary of these innovations have become indispensable to millions of us in our world today. Regarded as a genius on par with great innovative and influential inventors as Thomas Edison or Alexander

Graham Bell, who invented the telephone, Jobs was also an iconic figure as well as a successful executive. From its inauspicious origin in what has been described as the Silicon Valley, in his parents' Los Altos, California garage in 1976, Jobs managed to build his company Apple into one of the world's most valuable corporations in dollar terms today. The lives of so many of us have been irreversibly altered for the better by the innovations of Steve Jobs. Leaders get paid for generating ideas, dreaming up strategies and keeping the organization alive through strategic thinking. That's why they get paid much more than the regular staffers.

LEADING IN POLITICS

Politics is often described as a dirty game. Leading in politics can be very challenging. At the national level, citizens endeavor to vote in the right candidate to lead the nation to progress; and when the leader fails to deliver; the people will fire him by voting him out of office at the next elections. This is why democracy has come to be accepted as the best form of government where the people can choose their leaders and vote them out of office through a peaceful election. In a functional democracy, power flows from the ballot box rather than from the barrel of the gun. The people's mandate is very important to maintaining legitimacy in office.

During the partisan crisis that nearly shut down the United States of America government during President Obama's second term in office, he told the hardline GOP Tea Party members 'they should go out there and win an election' if they did not like the policies of the sitting president.

"*Neither the chains of dictatorship nor the fetters of oppression can keep down the forces of freedom for long*" -Angela Merkel

How true this is! Leaders do not command respect by the use of coercion or force, they rather influence their followers and earn their respect. That doesn't mean they are weak. They do not abandon their principles and views because of opposition or intimidation. They succeed irrespective of what goes on in the environment. You can't have a great idea without being challenged. They only place where people don't challenge each other is the graveyard. Leaders like Angela Merkel have succeeded in pushing through their reforms despite the opposition.

History has shown that no nation has made sustainable progress without a strong and visionary leadership. India, one of the oldest civilizations in the world today entered the 21st century with a population of more than one billion people. The nation, through strong leadership, is able to feed her people and has become a net exporter of food to other nations. Indians have equally advanced in technology, and ebbed a space for themselves with a strong military that possesses n nuclear weapons. India's indigenous car manufacturing industry has also begun to attract world attention.

The strong leadership provided by Sir Winston Churchill helped Great Britain survive the Second World War. And through effective leadership provided by the likes of Margaret Thatcher, the nation's strong economy was maintained, backed by a strong currency, the Pound Sterling. Thatcher was called the "Iron Lady" because of her firm and unbending belief in Britain.

"*If you want something said, ask a man. If you want something done, ask a woman.*"

"*Standing in the middle of the road is very dangerous; you get knocked down by the traffic from both sides.*"

"*Defeat? I do not recognize the meaning of the word.*" - Margaret Thatcher.

Such was the vigorous and incredible constitution of Thatcher - that's what leaders are made of. They must have a clear vision of where they're taking the rest of us to. And they have no apologies about their convictions.

In Singapore, Lee Kuan Yew is called 'the father of modern Singapore' because of his leadership acumen. In his book, *From Third World to First: The Singapore Story, 1965-2000,* he revealed how, by integrating technology into the country's economic and social system, Singapore was positioned to survive and succeed in the then fast emerging knowledge-based global economy. He was equally a highly principled leader with zero tolerance for corruption.

Deng Xiaoping, the leader of China modernization was a leader of vision. By 1978, China's per capita income was just around $40 with little progress to show with regard to food production. The amount of grain available per person in this communist state was less than it was in 1957. At the same time, the neighbouring countries referred to as "little dragons" - South Korea, Taiwan, Hong Kong and Singapore - were all experiencing spectacular economic growth. Deng saw that the future of China would be threatened, and the nation might become irrelevant in the near future, if it did not change its line of thinking. Under this climate, Deng's pragmatic calls for "professionalization" and economic reform found resonance among ordinary Chinese thus moving China nto the free market economy away from the ideologies of chairman Mao Zedong, who was a romantic idealist, unlike Deng, a pragmatic realist. Under Deng's leadership, markets were the key to China's modernization. Deng is remembered today as the leader who saved China through his pragmatic and visionary ideas. That is the essence of leadership - what comes out of your decisions. The world wants to see results not mere rhetoric.

CHAPTER THREE

STRATEGIC INNOVATION AND CHANGE MANAGEMENT

If you want to make enemies, try to change something.
- Woodrow Wilson

Change is inevitable because the world in which we live in is not static. Naturally, man hates and resist change, and would want the status quo to continue, especially when it guarantees continuity in the same comfort zone; until it becomes obvious that we have to change or be changed and left behind. When all our processes and strategies has run their course and we seem not able to continue the way we are, then we need to realize it is time to change our direction and move on. Doing this requires sometimes to change the drivers and doctors who previously managed the affairs and processes. Change can be painful sometimes, but it will come when it will come.

Change has been described as the adoption of an innovation (Carlopio, 1998: 2), where the main goal of the organization is to improve business outcomes or any other endeavour they may be involved with through an alteration of practices. However, it is true from practical evidence that the process of achieving change is complex, with very many different types of changes possible. Furthermore, there are a number of different strategies for adapting and implementing these changes with appreciable success. Each organization has to find out which of these models will work for its particular environment.

Alteration of processes is a key practice among change agents. Our methods, models and means must be subjected to constant review if we're to remain relevant. Change, they say, is inevitable. Innovation in almost everything we do and the need to sometimes change our methods of doing things has been with us right from the beginning of history; and has been and continues to be an important study on a number of levels. It plays a very significant part in economic growth as well as the survival and development of firms and businesses. New ideas, new products and new approaches become critical guidelines in organizational strategy, especially for top managers and business leaders. With a great vision, coupled with innovative ideas backed by willingness to learn and change, a little organization can become a big conglomerate.

More than 50 years ago, precisely on July 2, 1962, the very first Wal-Mart store was opened in the United States by Sam Walton in Rogers, Arkansas. Little did he know at that time that he was laying the foundation for an institution in America that would reshape not just business in the retail industry, but the United States itself and the world at large. About 4,400 stores later, and still counting, Wal-Mart's size, reach and influence truly boggles the mind. The organization has taken over as the world's largest private employer of labour. Only the United States

Department of Defense and the People's Liberation Army of the Republic of China employ more people than Wal-Mart. Wal-Mart's two million-plus workers exceed the population of some 15 states in the US and the District of Columbia. Come to think of it, every week, more than one hundred and forty million Americans shop at Wal-Mart - a figure that far surpasses the stadium audience of the 2012 Super Bowl or the number of voters who turned out during the 2008 US presidential elections.

Another organization that has helped change our world today is Apple Computers. Apple managed to overtake Coca-Cola and Google to become the world's most valuable brand in a group of 100 competitors in 2013, according to the New York-based corporate identity and brand-consulting company, Interbrand in its 2013 report on Best Global Brands.

Apple claimed the coveted top position that year, while Google and Coca-Cola secured the second and the third-place spots respectively. Coca-Cola had held the No. 1

position for thirteen consecutive years and now fell to third place.

Every so often, a company changes our lives- not just with its products but with its ethos. Innovation and adaptation allow organizations to introduce products that meet the needs of the future. It is not just sufficient to chase the available opportunities and fight fires.

A classic lesson to learn in the school of strategic innovation and change is Coca-Cola's answer to the notoriously and continuously unreliable distribution systems of developing countries. Instead of relying and using the existing traditional routes to market, Coke built its own network of smaller, local distribution centers, operated by entrepreneurs, who often use bicycles to distribute the product to the thousands of small shops and retail outlets in a given area. The innovation both helped to deliver Coke's 'always available' slogan and to provide substantial network of employment to the communities, thereby increasing its popularity. This is why today Coke can be found in the remotest village in Africa, South America and Asia. Muhtar Kent, President & Chief Executive Officer of Coca-Cola International, attributed the company's growth to the organization's 'adaptability to local markets.'

Factors that drive change itself may be internal or external to the particular environment (Credaro, 2006). Innovations often get initiated at any level in the organizational structure (Swenson, 1997) and reforms may be local or systemic in nature (Reigeluth, 1994).

Governmental organizations, commercial enterprises, service industries, non-profit organizations, and educational institutions all undergo change. Change is a continual process; if we refuse to change, we'll be changed.

THE CHANGE PROCESS

There are four basic steps in the change process:

a. Encouraging People for Change. The management of change is the very core activity in the drive towards realizing and achieving organizational goals, whilst implementation of new ideas is the physical and practical process of delivering an innovation. People and relationships are essentially the major components to successful implementation. Because people are the main obstacle to change, they have to be educated and encouraged to accept change so they can become the main catalyst for change. A good leader must find a way of turning followers into change agents.

b. Identifying Areas of Improvements. Identifying areas for improvement is the second stage in the implementation of the change process; this will be followed by the generation of possible solutions to addressing issues so identified. Activity in these areas should involve all the employees of the company as excellent ideas can come from the very lower cadre of staff. The days when managers are said to 'know it all' are clearly past. Young college undergraduates even school drop outs have been known to generate new ideas in business that have dazzled our world. Bill Gates, a Harvard drop out and Michael Dell are good examples here.

c. Implementation of Innovations. The third stage dwells on implementation of the innovations proposed. This is the most complex and difficult to achieve because it takes commitment and courage to change an existing system. In the school context, this may even be more difficult than in other organizations. Fullan (1993: 46) while commenting on the subject of teachers becoming change agents notes that educational reforms are "hard to conceive and even harder to put into practice." The process of implementing change is not linear (Carlopio, 1998: 5); it must progress from one stage to the other over the time, with real commitment from stakeholders together with common vision, shared decision-making collaboration and the putting in place of support structures.

Carlopio (ibid) notes that there are four stages the implementation stage of change normally goes through. The first step of implementation is:

1 The creation of "knowledge and awareness."

2 The second step in the implementation process in Carlopio's well-researched book, is the establishment of structures to facilitate change.

3 The third stage, the complex process of persuasion and engagement with decision and commitment; and lastly:

4 Rollout and fine tuning complete the implementation of the desired innovation.

To further show how difficult the implementation stage is, a study on business decisions reported that the success rate of implementation of innovations was only about 50% (Wind & Maine, 1998). The most successful practices, such as group problem solving, recorded the lowest rate of implementation whilst the least successful practices, like issuing directives, recorded the highest rate of implementation (Sauer, 1997).

d. Re-assessment and Re-evaluation. It is very necessary therefore that the implementation stage of change must be followed by re-assessment and re- evaluation with possibly further amendments needed so that issues of concern are identified and resolved. Honeywell Australia (1999) argued that change is "like fractal patterns", that is complex and iterative, with stakeholders in the organization reacting to each of the stages listed above by making "thousands of incremental adjustments."

INNOVATIONS IN HUMAN HISTORY

Humans are very ingenious species. From the primitive age when the early man used rocks commonly available on the ground to make the first sharp- edged tools, to the development and deployment of rovers to Mars and the creation of the Internet, several key advancements stand out in human history as particularly revolutionary. Man has not only been able to survive on land, ice and desert, man has visited even unfriendly space through innovations. Some of the weather conditions in some countries are so extreme that the inhabitants either innovate or perish. It can be argued that one of the factors that may have accounted for Africa's backwardness is the fact that a greater part of the continent enjoys weather conditions that are not life threatening. There is abundant sunshine and the continent has largely been spared from natural disasters compared to other regions where tsunamis, mudslides, hurricane and other violent storms, earthquakes together with extreme snow fall occur regularly. After the devastating effects of the atomic bombs dropped on Japan's Hiroshima and Nagasaki during World War 11, the country under those straits was stretched to innovate, the people's patriotism in those difficult days fueled by their belief in their country brought about Japan's economic rise to the second biggest until recently when behemoth China overtook them. Germany was equally almost completely destroyed during World War II when Berlin and other major cities were destroyed beyond recognition, thanks to the severe aerial bombardment and use of heavy weapons. The Germans equally rose from the rubble to build Europe's largest economy. Truth is: necessity continues to be the mother of innovations.

Temperatures in Antarctica could get as low as -40 degrees Fahrenheit during winter. Even animals and birds have to innovate to survive such extreme climate. Since the start of modern measurement in 1850, the world experienced unprecedented and extreme high impact climate during the period of 2001 to January, 2010 decade. According to World Meteorological Organization (WMC) in its report The Global Climate between 2001-2010 chronicled events such as heatwaves in Europe and Russia, Hurricane Katrina in the United States of America, Tropical Cyclone Nargis in Myanmar, serious bush fires in Australia, droughts in the Amazon Basin and the floods in Pakistan as very extreme and challenging to the survival of life generally. Yet, man continues to survive, and life went on through innovation in these areas.

Before the brilliant invention of the wheel in 3500 B.C., human beings were severely limited in how much materials they could transport over land, and how far they could transport them. When the wheeled carts came into use, it facilitated commerce and agriculture by enabling the transportation of heavy goods to and from markets, as well as assisting in the movement of people over great distances, thereby reducing the pain and burden of carrying heavy loads on our heads and shoulders.

Another area in human history where innovation became very useful was navigation. Since the oceans and seas account for about two-thirds of the entire earth space it became necessary to navigate the waters. Ancient mariners improvised by using the stars to navigate, but that method didn't work on cloudy nights or during the day and so it was unsafe in those days to voyage far from land.

The first compass was invented by the Chinese, sometime between the 9th and 11th century; the compass was made of lodestone, which is a naturally- magnetized iron ore, which they had studied for centuries. Soon after, the new technology passed on to the Europeans and Arabs through nautical contact. The compass became a very useful instrument; it enabled mariners to navigate safely far from land, which led to the increase in sea trade and contributed to the Age of Discovery. Today, we see very large ocean vessels conveying large quantities of goods and passengers across the oceans with ease. Japan used shipbuilding in the 1950s and '60s to rebuild its industria structure.

It is difficult to imagine the delay in reproducing documents and books if the printing press was not invented. German inventor, Johannes Gutenberg invented the printing press around 1440. Printing presses have exponentially increased the speed with which book copies could be made, leading to the rapid and widespread dissemination of knowledge across countries and continents. Millions of volumes of books and other printed materials are in circulation today due to this technology.

Time would fail us to talk about the telephone, the light bulb, the nail, the combustible engines, the aeroplane, and the space machines which have improved the quality of our lives today. Come to think of the internet; it really needs no introduction: The present global system of interconnected computer networks which is known as the Internet is used by billions of people worldwide. From available records, countless people helped to develop it, but the person most commonly credited with its invention is the computer scientist Lawrence Roberts who developed the initial works by other computer scientists to create what we now call the internet. It is impossible to outline its usefulness to the modern man today.

Africa is not left out. The Pyramids, which were built in the Fourth Dynasty in Egypt, testify to the power of the Pharaonic religion and state. These pyramids were built to serve both as grave sites as well as provide a way to make the names of the great people in Egypt at that time last forever. The size of the structures and their simple design show the high level of skill of the Egyptian engineers who designed them. How about the great works of art that continue to dazzle us today: good music and buildings which add to the beauty of our world. They all came as a product of the ever-creative mind of man as endowed by his Creator.

MANAGING CHANGE

An early model of change developed by Kurt Lewin (1951) described change as a three-stage process. The first stage (Unfreezing) involves overcoming inertia, fear and apathy and tackling the existing 'mind set', the second stage (Moving to the new level) is when change actually occurs. At the third stage (Refreezing), the new mind set is stabilized to prevent regression or backsliding to the old ways. Lewin's model appears too linear and simplistic to be applied in a complex environment like the African continent and other developing economies. A more workable transactional approach would have been more appropriate, this will involve the introduction of a feedback loop in the process, and such a process will also be dependent on the active involvement and cooperation of those at the bottom of the chain who will feel the impact of the change more. The preference for a bottom-up approach as compared to the traditional top-down approach, which the change agents in Africa seem to prefer is desirable, as it gives those at the bottom a sense of belonging, shared understanding and values. The era of know it all is over. Change is required in every society, old procedures must be turned into new processes, many observers agree with the phrase that the only condition permanent on earth is change, while accepting such principles, there are also those who argue that if a situation is good, then why change it, these are the people that readily cite the phrase 'if it is not broken, why fix it?' or 'why change a winning team?'. As true as all that may be, it is important for the winning team to keep on innovating and learning otherwise its competitors will gain the advantage and take over.

During World War II, the German U-Boats were invincible; they were the undisputable kings of the ocean; sinking thousands of Allied ships and killing many seamen on board the ships. Although the Germans had this advantage, little effort was made to modernize and improve the fighting capacity of the boat. Its main advantage was its ability to remain undetected underneath the sea. The design was left unchanged, the same model used during World War I without any improvements. This advantage continued from 1940 to 1943 when the Allied forces built ships with modern radars that could detect the U-Boats no matter how much they tried to maneuver. All the over 400 U-Boats were eventually sunk with over 30,000 seamen killed by Allied war ships and planes. The Germans lost the sea battles because they failed to innovate, and eventually lost the war. The lesson here is very clear; failure to innovate will lead to loss of advantage. And losing the advantage, brings competitors and contenders to the fore and top position.

INNOVATIONS AND CHANGE IN DEVELOPING NATIONS

Growing up in the mid-western part of Nigeria for me was very interesting. People here are deeply entrenched in the old ways. This is a region where the chief occupation is predominantly farming consisting mainly of tilling the ground with crude implements like cutlasses and hoes. Our high school geography and agricultural science teachers would tell us then that subsistence farming had become obsolete and that for our region to be self-sufficient and have enough for export we should start mechanized farming which involved the use of modern machines and scientific methods to boost crop quality and quantity. These lectures were taken just to pass the class tests and move ahead, there was very little change in terms of farm methodology till we left the village to the big cities in search of greener pastures.

The same is true of many geopolitical regions in Nigeria, West Africa and Sub-Sahara Africa in particular, and in most developing economies in our world in general. There are so many resources but few innovations to turn our volumes into value.

In 1990, it was speculated that about 82 million hectares out of Nigeria's total land area of 91 million hectares were arable. Yet, up till recently when I travelled the same old road across states like Ogun and Ondo to Edo, all in the western part of Nigeria to my village in the Mid-west, the vast acres of land are still lying fallow. One would drive for several kilometres without seeing a single commercial farm. From the car window, one could see plenty of fertile land without any agricultural activity taking place. Investment innovations in our vast lands alone without reliance on crude oil and other solid minerals could turn Nigeria into a superpower within a few years. Yet the contribution of crude oil and gas to the nation's earnings through export continues to account for more than 75% as at the early twenty-first century.

Occasionally, as we drove through the region, one encounters an old derelict lorry used by the illegal loggers who cut down trees and cart away our valuable wood outside the country which is latter returned as finished product in the form of foreign-made furniture which will then be sold to us at cut-throat prices. Why can't we harness these vast resources and produce things at home? One would ask.

People resist change. Persuading people to change from well tested, reliable, yet archaic methods is often difficult. This is because of the risk element in trying new things and employing new methods of doing things. The question that often went through my mind is: when change comes, are we really ready to embrace it?

Although many developing countries have started large scale and commercial farming which is beginning to engage the youths, there is still a long way to go when it comes to turning our volume of land into value. We must give room for more research and development in every sector of our economy, especially in the areas of agriculture and land development which nature has bestowed on us in very great abundance. We should not allow superstitions to take the place of scientific research and technological innovations.

Chinua Achebe, a popular literary giant and storyteller in his book *Things Fall Apart* quoted an Igbo proverb which states that: 'those whose palm kernels were cracked for them by a benevolent spirit should not forget to be humble.' This may not have been proven but it has worked for many, who believe in some benevolent spirits working behind the scenes to ensure success rather than face the reality that change has to be pursued with vigorous efforts. Can you imagine the head coach of a football team depending on 'benevolent spirits' without the help of a backroom staff and technical experts to win a competitive match? Or a CEO of a company who ignores cutting edge technology and best industry practices in favour of psychics and soothsayers invoking success without hard work? Such will be simplistic and wishful thinking.

But Africa has started to benefit from innovation and change. A little over a decade ago, there were only about 100,000 telephone lines in Nigeria, which were mostly landlines run by the state-owned telecoms giant, NITEL.

The phone lines were so erratic that you hardly could depend on them for good communication. Phone queues were very common in the '80's due to the limited number of phones. For those who enjoyed the 'luxury' of having telephones in their homes, had to cope with the added disturbance of having a considerable number of friends and relatives wanting to use the phone just to pass a message for a few minutes.

All that has changed; today, NITEL is dead, and Nigeria now has close to 100 million mobile phone lines, making it Africa's largest and fastest growing telecoms market, according to available statistics by the Nigerian Communications Commission.

Across the rest of the African continent the trends are very similar: between year 2000 and 2010, Kenyan mobile phone organization Safaricom saw a substantial increase in its subscriber base in excess of 500-fold. The number of mobile phone users in Rwanda grew by 50% in 2010 alone, as shown by figures from the country's regulatory agency.

During the early years of mobile phones in Africa, the Short Messaging Service (SMS) was at the centre of the revolution. People wanted to send cheap text messages to their loved ones but today, the next frontier for mobile users in Africa is the internet.

From October 2013, for the first time, the total number of Nigerians accessing the internet through their mobile phones grew and surpassed the number of desktop internet users in the country. The trend has continued that way since then. Most of the preferred devices are low-end Nokia phones, and other brands, tens of millions of which have already been sold out on the continent; in fact, the demand for phones in Africa is still increasing. The more expensive ones, the "smartphones," are, however, also increasing in popularity as their prices drop with middle income earners increasing. Blackberry's market share in Africa and the developing world has been on the rise, bucking the trend in North America and Europe until recently when the company started having problems.

Google, for its part, plans to sell 200 million Android phones in Africa, and there are estimates that by 2017 there could be a billion mobile phones on the continent, which is very huge.

President of Rwanda, Paul Kagame, said in 2007: "In 10 short years, what was once an object of luxury and privilege, the mobile phone, has become a basic necessity in Africa." CNN inside Africa report September 14, 2012.

To visualize what an African country will look like in 20 years, you'll need to sit in a college classroom in any of the countries today and listen to what the students are saying. The college campuses are the grounds where radical innovations and change most often occur in our world. Africa's future progress from poverty and backwardness, or the lack of it, is inextricably linked to what is happening in the universities and institutions of higher learning scattered all over Africa. Currently, though, only about 5 percent of the young people in sub-Saharan Africa attend colleges and other higher institutions of learning. This percentage is so small and worrisome, but they form the critical mass. You can be sure that the people to run the show in the future will be those few Africans in college right now. The figures are growing and interestingly, the girls are pouring into schools now more than ever before when they were denied the opportunity due to the discrimination that existed then. The future leaders in business and government- the professionals, lawyers, medical doctors, engineers, scientists and managers who will be responsible for tomorrow's infrastructure, education, primary and secondary health care, and other sectors - are currently sitting in a college classroom somewhere in Africa or outside Africa today. Nigerians for instance have great brains; their professionals are already accounting for a significant percentage of the workforce in Europe and America. Nigerians in diaspora are excelling all over the world in every field of human endeavor. This confirms that what is needed to ignite the Nigerian, and broadly, the African spirit is good and enabling environment created through effective leadership, and Africa will rise to the world stage.

The world's big multinationals and conglomerates are now beginning to see the huge opportunities in Africa, the continent is fast becoming a testing ground for breakthrough ideas and innovations, like high-tech products. With over 650 million mobile subscribers and still counting, it is no longer a place to be despised; no wonder so many expatriates, multinationals, entrepreneurs and educators are striving to tap from the continent's great potential. Without any gainsaying, Africa can be the next China in a few years from now with improved leadership and reduction in the security challenges. Improving access to the Internet and the relative and increasing ease of communication through cell phones is a clear indication of how the continent is adapting to, and adopting, new technologies by leapfrogging and overcoming the era of the landline. On a busy day in Lagos, Accra, Johannesburg and, even,

Freetown, you can find so many business owners shouting on their mobile phones in chauffeur driven cars. Africa has clearly opened a whole new world of growth through innovation and change with information at its core encouraging entrepreneurship and exceptional solutions for common issues.

Changing the world, especially Africa and the developing world, will take a little more time than we can imagine. It will take more time to correct more than a century's worth of bad business habits. How we overcome and expand will depend on how we evolve. Like John F. Kennedy said in his inaugural speech in January 20 1961, "... all these will not be finished in the first one hundred days, nor will it be finished in the first one thousand days... or even perhaps in our lifetime on this planet. But let us begin."

STABILITY IN LEADERSHIP

Nigeria will play a major role in African transformation. That is why many are praying and hoping for its stability and peace. Any civil or religious unrest in Nigeria will immediately produce Africa-wide problems due to her huge population. There is no country in Africa big enough to handle Nigerian refugees in case of any crisis with her over 170 million people.

Due to the obvious absence of government in many areas, people tend to fend for themselves and find ways and means to survive. Many end up setting up small scale businesses to cater for their needs and those of their loved ones. To succeed, it becomes necessary to understudy those who have succeeded in their various fields of endeavour. Many learn from them, sometimes spending as much as seven years of apprenticeship before 'graduating' to set up their own trade or businesses, still under the guardianship of their masters. And many more Nigerians depend on a meagre daily income to survive.

The nation has started to improve in many critical areas of human development. Lagos is currently undergoing a lot of changes under a succession of reform-minded governors. There have been giant strides in communication, IT and other areas. The power sector is currently in the process of privatization to stimulate the kind of revolution witnessed in the communication sector about ten years ago. This was contained in a presentation to the West African Power Industry Convention by Bolanle Onagoruwa Director General, Bureau of Public Enterprises in November 2011.

Nigeria still has her problems though. The culture of queuing for services does not presently exist in the country, be it at the petrol stations, banks, airports or retail shops. The queues I've seen are those apparently enforced; mostly by law enforcement agents. The military regime under General Buhari who served as Nigeria's Head of State from 1983 to 1985 was popular for its 'War Against Indiscipline' (WAI) an initiative that encompasses forced orderliness in the nation's open cities. Though many welcomed the results it produced, but most questioned the heavy-handedness of the military and police personnel used to enforce it. Most Nigerians are hardworking people, some, who work in government offices, come late to work and those who come early enough are so used to carrying out their duties in slow and sluggish paces that the customer needs are hardly met. All these problems are being addressed by the current government, though it is quite an onerous task. If the nation must progress it must reform. To tap the huge opportunities in the country, we must move away from the current over dependence on the oil sector and invest in agriculture where we have millions of acres of land to be put to economic use. And pay attention to the mining industry, which has been largely abandoned for many years now.

CHAPTER FOUR

LEADING DIVERSE TEAMS

"If we cannot now end our differences, at least we can help make the world safe for diversity."

- John F. Kennedy

The world is organized into leaders and followers. For any leader to succeed, he or she must possess the ability to work with people and together meet organizational goals. This implies working with a team of people from diverse places. And working in a diverse environment has its challenges, not least, managing differences. Some people are so difficult that working with them can be challenging. It's like an unequal yoke which inconveniences both partners. Yet others are so easy going that just about anyone can enjoy working with them. To get the best from people, the leader must equally be prepared to give his or her best.

One of the ways to get people from different backgrounds to work together in the same environment is through training. There is need to train and develop people in order to bring out the right skills in them. The ability to work with people is so vital to leadership success that every leader must develop skills in that area. Closely following is the need to train, educate and develop subordinates to do their jobs better.

Training is the acquisition of the right skill and technology that enables employees to perform their present jobs to a higher standard. It enhances human performance on the job the employee is presently doing or is being prepared to do. Training is an on-going process even after the employee has resumed duty. There may be need to extend the usefulness of the employee in the company by exposing him or her to other kinds of jobs. Training is different from education.

Education is training people to do a different kind of job. This is different from training, where employees attend courses or learning interventions and can be easily and fully evaluated immediately they return to work. The full benefit of education can be seen when the trained staff move on to their future jobs and are then tested on what they have learned. But not all trained and educated people are fully developed. Development is training people to go into completely new horizons or viewpoints with the application of new technology. It allows leaders to guide their organizations proactively into new expectations rather than fighting fires and reacting to changes already taking place in the industry. Staff, thus trained, educated and developed are encouraged to believe in teamwork among diverse contributors. To meet the present-day challenges from competitors in a fast growing, globalized and dynamic environment, organizations are reframing their hierarchical structures in such a way that employees achieve collectively rather than doing things alone (Nansen and Nohira, 2004). The team leader must possess the right skills to influence the right actions from the other nembers of the team, which requires planning and nnovation.

What is in vogue now is participatory leadership. Any organization that continues to create a system around one know-it-all-entrepreneur may not compete well under the current business environment. It is always more advantageous to brainstorm around issues, select the best options and implement them after they've been sufficiently challenged in a team of diverse contributors. Wonderful ideas can be generated through this medium; and ideas, howbeit, good ideas, they say, rule the world. This does not create a situation where the involvement of so many cooks spoils the broth. The leader will still provide leadership but incorporates useful ideas from subordinates.

A very good example is the football team where collective effort will be required to win the match. Each player has something to contribute to the overall success of the team. They either succeed together or fail together.

DEFINITION OF DIVERSITY

Diversity is all about empowering people to contribute to organizational success. It makes an organization more effective by harnessing the collective strengths of each staff without exception.

Diversity means variety. The concept encompasses respect and acceptance of others' views. It comes from the understanding that every individual is unique and has something important, maybe different to contribute to the overall success of any endeavour. Diversity takes into consideration that we can achieve through our differences. The bringing together of people of different gender, race, ethnicity, religious beliefs, political convictions, orientations and ideologies produces a very colourful effect. It encompasses the need to understand each other, tolerate, embrace and celebrate each other's abilities.

Business organizations are including diversity and inclusiveness policies in their workplaces today in order not to be left behind. Inclusiveness means we value respect and appreciate people who don't look, think, act or speak like us. And when we find ourselves working with such people in the same organization, we do not discriminate against them in any way, or try to show open or covert resentment to their persons.

Those who have realized the power of diversity will always tell you that two heads are better than one. And like we have already discussed in the introduction, two good, well trained, educated and developed heads are better than one. The question then is: under what conditions are two heads better than one? And when do too many cooks spoil the broth?

Certainly, all big restaurants have many cooks working for them. So having lots of cooks won't spoil the broth, if all of them are following the same recipes. The chaos comes about if they are not in agreement and therefore follow different recipes and methods at the same time. In fact, having plenty of cooks is necessary to running a great restaurant.

When it comes to solving organizational problems, like coming up with a new product or finding ways to improve our service, ideas come faster from a diverse team where people with diverse experiences work together.

OPENING UP THE IDEA OF DIVERSITY

One of the useful things we should immediately learn about diversity is that is has various dimensions. There are cognitive differences in people, not just in the area of gender, ethnicity, religion or race but about differences in interpretations, dimensions, heuristics and predictions. People have different ways of representing problems and situations that confront them. They put things in different classifications and categories. People come up with different interpretation to what others do. One person can conclude that another person is aggressive while someone else will, in fact, appreciate that same person's assertiveness and see it as a positive talent that should be developed and utilized. Some people can write down solutions but do a poor job when it comes to explaining how it will work. Others are very good with talking and making their points clear but are poor writers. Some others, still are very good thinkers who can easily generate ideas and paint the big picture. Some people get their inspiration better when the music is playing in the background while others will prefer a serene environment and regard the music as a distraction and a noise.

The challenge is to put all these different people together in a team and bring out the best in them.

WHAT EXACTLY DOES DIVERSITY INCLUDE?

Diversity does not discriminate against people; male or female, black and white, young or old, fast learner and slow learner, extrovert or introvert, conservative or liberal. Diversity is about helping people realize that it requires a wide variety of people to bring out the best team. An organization requires the services of thinkers, controllers, team builders and dreamers, to reach their very best.

We must understand the current need for minorities and women to step into leadership roles. It is such marginal groups that have not been sufficiently explored who interestingly have much to offer. Every player in the corporate environment that aspires to get to the top must be prepared to accommodate and incorporate diversity in its leadership mix. Such leaders must first demonstrate that they have the talents to bring about growth and innovation.

DIVERSITY AND INNOVATION

We can foster innovation through a diverse workforce. People from different backgrounds approach problems from different viewpoints. With their collective range of knowledge and experience which they bring into the work, they can produce better services or finished products.

When people are given opportunity to speak on the same subject, their approach will be different from each other, which will bring about a cocktail of solutions to the problems that confront the organization. Diversity can affect group outcomes with regard to performance and innovation. In a study carried out at Kellogg School of Management at Northwestern University, Evanston, Chicago, it was discovered that diverse groups performed better than homogenous ones, not because of the influx of new ideas, but because diversity triggered more careful information analysis that is absent in the homogenous situation.

Under a school environment, diversity can foster better collaboration with other institutions leading to improved research for the benefit of the students. Diversity makes the organization a more rounded place. Many top organizations prefer bringing in tested outsiders to fill top vacancies because they bring with them experience from the outside which can help grow the organization.

Diversity in teams creates multiple benefits. For instance, when people work together collectively, one person in the team might suggest an improvement which, when built upon by others, makes the idea even better and richer. One plus one here will often produce a sum that is more than two. This is why organizations often consider bringing in outsiders to work with the existing team in the company to stimulate growth through injection of new ideas. These new intakes are not just highly paid consultants in fancy suits who come to add their own layers to the good decisions already taken by the in-house directors, but they are people who can bring in experience and relevant perspectives from competitors and even adversaries in the industry. One way to derive more advantages from diverse teams is to first define the goal and agree on it. If we first agree on the goal then disagreements and different opinions about the way to reach the goal can be helpful in expanding the array of solutions available to choose from. Getting problems solved through diversity in a team that s fundamentally different will require compromise to achieve the objective of the company, not just stereotyped to drum home the views of a dominant team member.

Next, it will be important to create an organizational culture where all employees are valued and allowed to contribute freely. By defining our organization as one that encourages and promotes diversity and inclusiveness is enough to give us an edge. Using terminologies like 'junior staff', 'non-core staff' and 'management,' 'senior' or 'expatriate staff' can create barriers to bonding and integration in the workplace. Having a separate restaurant for various categories of workers can bring about inferiority complex. The design of the work environment should allow people who are physically challenged access to facilities that makes them feel welcome and accepted. The restrooms for instance should not be segregated in such a way that racial prejudice is suspected. Finally, there will be need to acquire the right technology that encourages diversity and inclusiveness.

THE CHALLENGE OF EMBRACING DIVERSITY

To realize the full advantages of diversity there is need to first grow the workforce from groups into teams that utilize the full potential of every person involved. Teams have an advantage over groups. A group is made up of individuals where each person involved works towards his or her own goal; while a team involves a collection of individuals who work towards a common vision or goal. This helps the organization to create a synergy effect within the teams; meaning one plus one will produce more than two. A tree cannot make a forest. An individual who acts alone, can achieve much; but a group of people working together on the same project in a unified force can accomplish greater results. This is because team members understand and support one another. Their main objective is to collectively achieve their mission. Personal or selfish agendas do not get in the way of the collective drive and interest of the team. By using the synergy created in teams there will be a competitive advantage over other organizations within the industry or outside where people act alone and work against each other.

One of the main obstacles to teamwork is the fear of change. People can be so settled with the old system of one 'Sergeant Major' calling the shots and dictating from the top that they can't see a different model. Others resist change because of sentiments, tribalism and favouritism. These challenges have always been there. It is when we eventually come to realize that diversity is the key for turning our weak areas into strength does the group begin to grow and realize its full potential. If we fail to accept the diversity of others we'll continue to keep the group members from going after team objectives.

WHY EMBRACING DIVERSITY IS A CHALLENGE

Individual bias and prejudice are deeply rooted within some of us.

It will be necessary to train our staff on the importance of diversity in order to erase the existing bias on people's minds. This problem won't go away after a quick training on diversity. There is need for informal engagements of people who need that extra push to embrace change. Should this fail, it will become necessary to exclude those who feel strong about the old ways from the team. Embracing and accepting diversity is more than just tolerating people who are different; it requires actively involving and welcoming them by:

- Creating and developing a working atmosphere that is safe for all employees to ask for and get help from others in their team. People should not be seen as weak just because they ask for help. This is exactly what helps to build great teams - blending weakness with strength to have the objective accomplished.
- Deliberately and actively seeking for information from people of diverse cultures and backgrounds in order to make progress.

'f an organization does not accept the challenge of diversity, it stands the danger of becoming extinct and being left behind in a fast growing and competitive world. Customers do not welcome or tolerate substandard service, they want the best, and, therefore, they will move to other organizations that are customer oriented. Great companies who strive to remain at the top know there are others who want to overtake them; therefore, they put in a lot of efforts to remain competitive.

THE ROLE OF CULTURE

Harnessing the full advantage of diversity in our workplaces is not without its challenges. There are perpetual attitudinal barriers that we must cross. For diversity programs to take root and succeed in our work environment, we must overcome language, cultural and personal barriers that can jeopardize our efforts at implementing and harnessing the full benefits of team work. We'll always have a few employees in the system that will refuse to accept changes in the social and cultural makeup of their workplaces. To implement diversity there must be continuous communication of its benefits with training efforts to change staff mentality in the workplace. We will however find out that training alone is not enough; there must be a strategic plan in place to see it through till it becomes entrenched. Reviews can be carried out through periodic assessment of the diversity process as part of the management system. This will help determine which changes need to be put in place and the obstacles to diversity that are still present in the workplace for which appropriate policies will be needed to eradicate.

The personal commitment of the management team is a must. Managers and leaders within the organization must inculcate and incorporate the existing policies on diversity into every aspect of the organization's purpose and function. Diversity attitudes originate from the top where they are cascaded to the last man in the team.

Effectively leading the world of today and the world in the foreseeable future requires people who can understand, recognize and embrace and value the strength in differences. The world has become a global village therefore, it will take a whole village to produce the best. This is what is required to build the critical success in the new century.

To begin with, we must first make efforts to know ourselves better. There is a great potential in discovering who we are and the baggage we bring from our past; this is what is referred to as self-discovery. After discovering ourselves, we make efforts to know other members of the team better. We cannot fail to see the link between productivity and knowledge. Knowledge about their strengths and weaknesses, the opportunities they generate and the threat they pose to the growth of the organization, if any. After this stage, we begin to highlight their strength over their weaknesses and their potential over the problems they create. For most of us, this process of knowing ourselves and others better continues throughout our lives. An essential component of our personal and professional integrity is our belief system. This forms our values, attitudes, motives, actions, skills, talents and abilities. These are the perceptions that form and influence the relationship we have with others in our teams.

Since our attitudes are very deeply rooted, they are always very hard to change. As we stated before, changing attitudes is extremely difficult. To change the attitude of people, there'll be need to evolve a training method that changes the behavior, and this will take quite some time. Getting great results from a team is not just about getting everyone to come to a quick agreement on all the issues, the breakthrough comes from the collaboration of different thinking styles put together.

MANAGING DIVERSITY.

Coming back to the Nigerian experience, we learn a lot about diversity. It's impossible to live and work in Nigeria without having to learn how to manage diversity. Just by living in such a diverse environment teaches enough lessons about diversity. My country, Nigeria is a very diverse country with over two hundred ethnic groups and languages. Ethnicity and Religion are the two issues that have played a dominant role both in our way of life and governance. Since the nation is already almost equally divided between the Muslim North and the Christian South, all activities and actions of government are clothed in the garment of religious and ethnic differences. This is what brought about the quota system (which is our own version of the American affirmative action) that blocks out a quota of opportunities for religions and ethnic reasons. In our presidential system, a Muslim will have to be the vice president if the president is a Christian and vice versa. This has made it impossible for the best to compete for opportunities as others with less potential must be considered otherwise you begin to hear about marginalization of a certain zone or region. That is why (Enwerem, 1995) and (Dlakwa, 1997) have argued that the political behaviour of some Nigerians is heavily influenced by the hyperbolic assumption that one's destiny is exclusively and intrinsically linked with one's religious or ethnic group.

Nigeria is the most populous country in Africa and the most populous black nation in the world with a population of over 170 million people; which could be well over 200 million when the next census is taken. The problems of the country can be traced back to the colonial times when people of very diverse religious, social and ethnic backgrounds were brought together as strange bed fellows to form a country. Before the creation of Nigeria as a country, there were various empires and kingdoms such as the Benin kingdom, the Oya empire of the Yorubas, the Fulani emirate, the Hausas, Urhobo and many others. All his changed with the conquest of Lagos in 1861 by the British imperialists and the subsequent amalgamation of northern and southern Nigeria in 1914. After a lot of struggle, Nigeria gained independence in 1960, but the problem of ethnicity and religious differences continued up till present times. Successive governments, both democratic and military, have struggled under this yoke for years without finding the right way to the desired Eldorado. Leadership has been a problem from inception.

There are a lot of lessons that can be learnt from Nigeria's experience in managing ethnic and religious diversity.

Nigeria's diversity has posed a lot of challenges to its governance as seen from the many ethnic and religious conflicts we have had to manage. At the present moment, there are a lot of efforts being made to tackle these challenges and there are lessons other countries can learn from the Nigerian experience.

The way forward is to harness the benefits of our diverse structure instead of focusing on the issues that divide us.

There is need to understand each other and convert our differences into strength. This is the whole essence of diversity and inclusiveness. And instead of heaping all the blame on the British colonial imperialists, we should harness the advantage in our strength and take the world. And since we already have the size and a legion of people, there is a huge advantage in harnessing the human and material capital to our advantage.

LESSONS

From our discussion under this topic, we can deduce that understanding and respecting the diverse views of other people can produce the desired innovation and growth in every organization. Going solo and acting unilaterally has its advantages, but the benefits of harnessing the ideas, experiences and contribution of others cannot be overemphasized.

Actions that can create barriers to bonding and integration of the workforce or lead to inferiority complex should be avoided. Even the design of the work environment should allow people who are physically challenged to feel welcome and accepted.

It's a known fact that culture and attitude of people can form a big barrier to diversity, but effective training and a clear commitment from the management team will bring about the desired results in about any organization.

We must understand the current need for minorities and women to step into leadership roles especially in Africa, where the women are culturally given secondary roles. The basis of enhancing relationship, regardless of the culture from which we come from and in which we live are respect, trust and shared goals. We must trust that what a man can do a woman can do even better.

Learning to place a great value on diversity, to become very conscious of our ways of relating to each other, is not something easy to most of us; nor is it something that can be very quickly imposed from the outside. When we work hard at it we will discover, like so many others, that together we do it better.

CHAPTER FIVE

BUSINESS ETHICS AND SUSTAINABILITY

"In matters of style, swim with the current; in matters of principle, stand like a rock."

- Thomas Jefferson

INTRODUCTION

Ethics is about a person's decisions about right or wrong. It is a kind of philosophy that determines what a person believes to be morally good or

bad. There are disagreements about where personal ethics originated from. Some philosophers use man's sense of morality to support the existence of God to direct and influence man to do what is right, uphold justice and do to others what he expects others to do to him. They believe that these ethical qualities are instilled in humankind by God which in turn created a universal system of the acceptable and the unacceptable, the right and the wrong. This school of thought believes that the effect of one's religious orientation is the foundation for good morality and that morality cannot exist or flourish outside of religion.

Those who do not see the connection between religion and ethics may argue that people who are not involved with any religion often behave well and have good ethical standards and policies governing their lives. Evolutionists have their own explanation about the origin of ethics. They argue that personal ethics in humanity is about survival of the fittest. They teach that from the foundation, species that place little value on life probably killed off themselves gradually, while species with much ethical value were given greater opportunity to reproduce since they frown on murder and violence. Evolutionists believe that man genetically inherited the ability to discern between right and wrong that are to the society's advantage.

Other philosophers argue that ethics are not inherited from parents but are a product of children simply learning from their parents, friends, teachers and others what is right or wrong. In order words, whatever these children see and observe to be common in a given environment, they simply imbibe. The story talks about a boy who when asked why he was fighting with his brother simply replied 'we are acting mummy and daddy' because their parents were in the habit of fighting and quarrelling. Values and ethics is the yardstick to determine and shape how two people will see the same situation or circumstance. One may say it is right, the other may say it is wrong. Social and personal ethics relate to the degree of integrity and honesty in people. The code of ethics is important in life both personally and professionally.

Ethics in business means doing the right thing, taking the right course. In order to act ethically, a business organization must take into account every bit and every factor of doing business. These will include all the business processes from start to the end, from the production of goods and services to the working environment and conditions. From the corporate attitude to host communities in the areas of operation, to the strategy it employs in distribution and marketing of its products. It is a holistic decision to always do the right thing in everything the company does and to do all within the power of the organization to uphold the interests of others in the operating areas.

Sustainable development on the other hand is simply about doing business in such a way that we leave something behind for the generations coming after us. This is what some refer to as a balanced and enduring approach to all economic activity; being responsible environmentally and creating benefits for the society where we operate. There is no way business activity will not impact upon the environment. Even animals seeking pasture impact on the environment, but there is a whole world of difference between impacting on the environment and devastating it. Sustainable development is about ensuring that our future generations can indeed enjoy the same kind of lifestyle that we currently enjoy today. Naturally, this will involve putting into consideration the long-term effect of what we are doing today and balancing our economic gains with the environmental and human wellbeing of our society. It is a requirement in some countries that a business organization demonstrate a commitment that it will behave ethically and practically. They are required to show their commitment to Corporate Social Responsibility (CSR) as a business policy. There are national and international bodies whose responsibility it is to ensure that CSRs are in place and that the business activities and processes indeed take them into account. Business organizations who are found not be, have put in place standard ethical and sustainable development policies and practice are either shut down or rated low, which, in itself, is an indictment on the organization.

Public anger is vexed on such organizations that are not committed to ethical behavior and sustainable development. Sustainable development also involves putting the environment back in shape after necessary economic activities are allowed to impact substantially on it. This will involve remedial steps like planting new trees after the existing ones have been uprooted or cut down, soil remediation after an oil spill, cleaning up the ocean after an economic activity may have impacted negatively upon it. This is done with or without compulsion from the government and people living in that environment.

BUSINESS REPUTATION

The reputation of a business unit or organization is very essential to its survival and progress. The confidence and trust of the consumer can have a profound and direct effect on the bottom line of the company. In recent times, the significance of reputation has become a front burner issue to businesses and organizations. From managers and leaders of big conglomerates and multinational organizations to small businesses, churches and clubs, the need to cultivate their responses to crises occurring in their areas of operation cannot be over emphasized. This is necessary in order to salvage, maintain or improve their reputation and standing in the minds of the public.

In those days, businesses relied more on the word of mouth while dealing with their stakeholders. In this modern *show me* world, a business organization has to go further from *read my lips* to *read my actions* in order to maintain its place in the hearts of customers and consumers. These are the days of social networking, internet, smart phones and other methods of instant sharing of information; and for a business or any organization to have a chance, it must be conscientious in its dealings and be responsive to any crisis that may have any impact on its reputation.

Having a good reputation may look like an intangible concept or idea, but the benefits can be harvested in multiple ways. Once the consumers express their preference for a product or determine to support it, they may help defend the company as silent ambassadors whenever there is a controversy or a crisis which might otherwise erode public confidence - all these will have a direct or indirect effect on the market value and market share of the company.

If an organization maintains an excellent reputation in the marketplace, consumers will choose the product of that company ahead of others who may sell at a lower price. The reputation of a company creates room for a company to differentiate its products especially in highly competitive markets. It will allow the company the opportunity of selling at a better price and may become the ultimate factor in the decision of a consumer patronizing one business over another.

Research has confirmed, for example, that due to an increase in awareness and demand for healthy and more environmentally friendly food, efforts are being made by companies to label their products and display their quality to customers who are willing to pay a higher price for brands and labels that are considered to have maintained more of a prestigious and respectable reputation than others.

A study carried out in America identified ten parameters people use in measuring the reputation of an organization. These are:

a. Ethics: the public belief that the organization behaves ethically and is admirable and trustworthy.

b. Workplace/Employees: the public have come to believe that the organization has brought together talented employees, and that they treat people well, respect customers and operate in a healthy and conducive workplace.

c. Financial performance: the organization is strong financially; has been quite profitable and has great prospects for growth.

d. Leadership: the organization is a leader in the industry, not just a follower. It is perceived to be innovative.

e. Management: the quality of the leader (CEO, MD, etc.) plays a very vital role in how well the company is received. If it is believed that such a leader has turned the company around and has a clear vision for the future, the value of its shares may rise.

f. Social Responsibility: the organization accepts its social responsibility and has strongly convinced the customers, consumers and stakeholders about that. Lawsuits that have merit are attended to, and people whose rights have been inadvisably violated are settled in cash or kind.

g. Customer focus: the organization is customer friendly; cares about them and is very committed to their issues. When products are returned after sales because the customers have issues with them, they given attention, with their rights upheld.

h. Quality: the belief that the organization offers high quality services or products.

i. Reliability: the organization is ready to defend its products and services anywhere, and is consistent.

j. Emotional appeal: It's fun to do business with the organization; I feel good about it. All that could generate a lot of value.

To improve the value of the organization, especially in the eyes of the outside world, a number of things can be done: trust must be built and established by paying vendors as at when due, providing excellent services and keeping promises to customers. The habit of returning calls to enquirers can go a long way in shaping their view of the organization. Paying attention to details, and accepting balanced criticisms are very key to winning hearts and minds. Being sensitive to the needs of your customers (who are the life blood of the organization) and keeping the company's side of the deal is a step in the right direction.

Effective communication is a very good way to win public support. Do not wait for negative information to circulate before coming out with your own side of the story. In the event that accidents or other disasters occur, it is always good to show that the organization is deeply pained by the incident and that it puts the lives of its employees and members of the public ahead of profit.

ASSESSING ENVIRONMENTAL IMPACT IN BUSINESS

Managing the organization' s impact on the environment enhances financial benefits while making the company look responsible. To achieve this, there must be a conscious effort to ensure that environmental impact assessment is carried out at the beginning. Where necessary, experts from outside should be engaged in carrying out the job in order to boost public confidence.

This is necessary so that the result will not be seen as an insider job. It is also ethically correct to pull out of an area where operations will destroy sensitive species in the existing water bodies and ecosystem.

ENVIRONMENTAL MANAGEMENT PLANS

Environmental management strategies should be incorporated into the business plan. As part of the planning, an environmental audit is necessary to help determine which areas of the business impact on the environment, and the degree of the impact. It will then be good to include environmental management plans and methodology in the daily operations of the company or organization.

To protect the business and the environment under which it operates, there is need to find out if the business activities fall under the category for environmental licensing or legislation. Certain goods or appliances imported or manufactured in certain countries need to comply with environmental standards before they can be sold to the public. Each of these standards spells out a rating and labeling stamp to direct consumers on how well a product uses a resource from the environment, which has the additional benefit of promoting suppliers and producers of such products.

ETHICAL BUSINESS PRACTICE IN DEVELOPING ECONOMIES

In many developing economies today, issues bordering on business ethics and sustainable development are fast attracting the attention of the public. In the primitive days, where the level of awareness was so low among communities living in the jungles of Africa, Asia and Southern America, business organizations, especially in the extracting industries went into forests and virgin lands to explore and extract natural resources like crude oil, diamond, gold, granite stones, marble and limestone, to mention but a few. The only compensation that came to the ignorant host communities in those days was in the form of building cassava processing plants, construction of poor-quality blocks of classrooms and boreholes for potable water, for which the chiefs and rulers of those communities were very grateful.

This same ignorance prevailed during the trans- Atlantic slave trade, where young boys and girls, men and women were sold off into slavery to Europe, America and West Indies in return for ephemeral gifts like umbrellas, hot drinks, snuff and jewelry. Some narrow roads were constructed into the jungles just wide enough to transport raw materials like timber, granite, fish, palm oil, cotton, coffee, kola nuts, groundnuts and millet to the seaports where they are then exported outside of our shores, with the ignorant communities dancing and rejoicing that development has come by the road construction.

However, as civilization came with education, the cost of doing business in these developing communities steadily rose although labor costs in developing economies are relatively cheaper. Even though ethical standards are now being put in place, it is still very possible to obtain production licenses and contracts from corrupt government officials after paying just a little bribe.

There are many companies doing business in Africa today who can still evade tax and employ cheap labor who work under inhuman conditions simply because the authorities in those places failed to hold them to account. That does not imply that progress has not been made. There is an increasing awareness in the developing economies about the ethical behavior of local and international organizations doing business in those countries.

The most common of the ethical issues we're dealing with today in the developing economies borders on issues like working standards and conditions, corruption, child labor and gender equality. Many organizations operating in those economies are developing their own systems of dealing with those ethical issues and are making steady progress.

WORKING STANDARDS AND CONDITIONS

With the rising labor costs in Europe and America, and the need for employers to exploit places where affordable labor might be found, we have witnessed in recent times big corporate organizations shifting their business wholesale to Asia and Africa. Those who do not maintain their presence in those areas often offload some of their jobs there through the process of outsourcing. While profits may rise through affordable labor it is clear that workers across the globe will suffer the most. Workers in some of these countries are working under poor conditions. Under those conditions, workers are made to work long hours, throughout the week including Sundays without opportunity to even go to church. They may be paid what is referred to as 'overtime pay' but it is essentially a paltry sum when compared to the deprivations the workers suffer. Others are made to work in factories that are unsafe and unhealthy where they are exposed to all kinds of diseases.

Employers must always be aware of the safety of their work environments, they must equally be concerned if they are keeping staff on jobs for unnecessarily long hours or if they are engaged in unusually difficult tasks, like doing jobs which are suited for machines and robots. There are legal consequences for unethical behaviour both from employers and employees. Business owners must always determine whether it is ethical to outsource or do business with suppliers and partners who are involved with unethical practices.

CORRUPTION IN BUSINESS

Some writers commenting on the subject of corruption say that corruption is present in all governments, and that it is not something that is peculiar or limited to any region, continent, ethnic group or nationality. It is a problem which is present in every political, economic and social system in the world, and affects the young and the old, men and women alike. It is something that is found in countries that are democratic as well as those that are more or less dictatorial in nature. Capitalist economies, socialist and feudal systems are bedeviled by corruption in diverse forms. Such writers equally canvas that corruption is as old as the world; in other words, it did not begin today. Ancient civilizations we read about in our history books all have traces of widespread corruption and illegality. Therefore, corruption has been present in complex societies from ancient Egypt, Rome, Israel and Greece down to our present age. (Upset and Lenz,2000: 112-113). This does not, however, suggest or conclude that the magnitude or extent of corruption is equal in every society. Some countries are manifestly more corrupt than others!

Corruption involves the setting aside of rules that had been established for personal advantage or gain (Sen, 1999:275). Corruption is practiced when one seeks to secure power, wealth or advantage through illegal and fraudulent means at the expense of the general public. It is a misuse of the authority or trust given by the public in order to benefit privately (Upset & Lenz, 2000:112- 114).

In addition, corruption is behaving in a way which deviates from the formal duties of a public role, because of selfish private gain. It includes such behavior as bribing others to pervert justice or bend the rules (Nye, 1967). To add to the already crowded landscape, Banfield (1961) adds that it is an illegal appropriation of resources belonging to the public for private use. Osoba (1996) posited that corruption is an anti-social behaviour seeking to confer improper benefits contrary to the moral and legal norms existing in a given society of organization and which, in effect, reduces the living conditions of the people.

To combat corruption in our nations and workplaces, we must develop a culture of relative openness in managing relationships with contractors and customers. Existing ethical and sustainability laws should be strengthened. Companies and organizations applying to do business in developing economies should be made to sign on to and commit themselves to high ethical behaviour both in their workplaces and in their business policies. Finally, there should be stiff penalties imposed through our legal systems to ensure organizations that violate ethical and sustainability rules do not go unpunished.

CHAPTER SIX

EFFECTIVE ORGANIZATIONAL THEORY AND PRACTICE

"It is essential that there should be organization of labor. This is an era of organization. Capital organizes and therefore labor must organize".

- Theodore Roosevelt

An organization is a unit or a system where people and resources are striving to obtain pre-determined objectives. An organization may be a production plant, a marketing unit, a service delivering entity, a church or a social club, which requires people and resources for its sustenance. In addition to people and resources, an organization requires another essential element to direct these resources to their proper ends: Management.

Management is as old as man. It became necessary from the time men began to form social organizations. As the world is made up of leaders and followers, someone must direct and lead the way to the desired end. Managing people was very simple in the early days of human existence, it required leaders with just natural talents and ability to lead to direct and coordinate the primitive economies of those times - primarily made up of subsistence farming, hunting, fishing and animal husbandry. However, as the world's population began to multiply and organizations became more and more complex in a dynamic world, theories of management became essential in order to understand how this ever-increasing task of managing people and organizations can be done. But, let's begin by defining the term management.

DEFINITION OF MANAGEMENT

Management can be defined as the process by which human, financial, physical and informational resources are used to attain the objectives of the company. Management is about working with people and utilizing the available resources to achieve set objectives.

Koontz and Weihrich, McGraw-Hill, 1990 defined management as "the process of designing and maintaining an environment in which individuals, working together in groups, efficiently accomplish selected aims." Management can be broken down into four components: planning, organizing, directing and controlling. These activities do not stand alone by themselves, they relate with each other and involve elements of motivation and delegation and, above all, their successful implementation depends on good communication. Managers delegate authority a lot in order to groom leaders for the future.

If you pick the right people and give them the opportunity to spread their wings - and put compensation as a carrier behind it - you almost don't have to manage them." - Jack Welch

FUNCTIONS OF MANAGERS

Let's examine the functions of Managers in a more detailed way:

1. Planning

The adage goes that if you fail to plan you are planning to fail. Planning is very important in the management process. It is concerned with setting the goals of the company and determining how and by whom they should be achieved. The start point is the vision - a mental picture of where you want to be in the future considering the resources available. There is need to write down various options and alternatives to achieving the goals already set. A decision will then be made effectively backed up with necessary budgets and commitments. A good plan will be time-bound and must include the action party and the detailed responsibility to be carried out.

2. Organizing

Organizing will logically follow after the plan has been put in place. It is the work that managers must do to put the plan into effect. It involves a proper assessment of what resources are available - comparing what you have on the ground with what is actually needed to get the work done. It will then be necessary to distribute the work according to the several abilities of the workers who must work to deliver on their goals. Since management involves working with people to achieve set objectives the right establishment has to be put in place specifying who does what, how and when. The organization will need to be designed and the process of finding the right people to fit into the various jobs. Placing them and motivating them by way of additional responsibilities, remuneration and promotion will be done and it is not an easy task. Since it is difficult to manage people, managers will develop their leadership abilities to fulfill their roles.

3. Directing

Leading involves motivating and influencing people to follow. If you are going somewhere as a leader and nobody is following, you are probably taking a walk. Leaders must have the ability to influence people to want to follow them. Meeting deadlines is an important factor in whatever we are doing. The manager must therefore have the necessary influence to get subordinates to meet organizational deadlines.

4. Controlling

Since managers are concerned about meeting the organizational standard, they have the responsibility of controlling their subordinates to be sure that what they are doing conforms to the standard of the organization. It is common to hear managers in the various industries talk about the standard of their organizations; and they take the pain to explain this to every new staff joining the organization to foster compliance.

Management functions cannot be limited to the internal environment alone, managers must operate in the external environment of an organization as well. Clearly, managers cannot perform their tasks well unless they have an understanding of, and are responsive to, the many elements of the external environment - economic, technological, social, political, religious and ethical factors - that affect their operation.

GOALS OF ALL MANAGERS

The aim of managers is to achieve what the organization sets out to do with the available resources - human and material. In order to maintain profitability and market share, the manager must control costs and maximize profits for its shareholders or owners. Goals differ from organization to organization. There are some organizations that prefer to remain small for fear of expansion. Many organizations in Nigeria and in many other countries in

Africa contend with the problem of access to capital needed for expansion, they will therefore set goals to the limit of their equities - what the owners of the business can afford together with financial help from friends and relatives.

Another goal of managers is to improve productivity. This involves setting targets at the beginning of the business year and ensuring those targets are met or even exceeded at the end of the business year. The effectiveness and efficiency of the staff involved is very key to achieving these goals. It is also important to avoid wastages and work 'within budget' as some people like to call it. It can be added that managers aim at satisfying customers and consumers, and to do this effectively, knowledge of consumer behaviour in a given environment becomes very useful. Managers delegate duties to subordinates and arrange for staff progression in their organizations. To boost the morale of staff and recognize hard work, promotion comes in. It is however important to balance the need to elevate the staff with that of keeping the staff on the job where he or she can best contribute to the growth of the organization. The reason for this is because success in one role is not always an indication of success in another. Consider how many account representatives fail woefully when they are promoted to sales managers. The ability to sell is entirely distinct from the ability to manage. Promotion may then remove an account representative from where she has been contributing substantially to the value for the company into a new job where she is unable to neither cope nor make impact.

WHY STUDY MANAGEMENT THEORY?

Human behaviour is the result of needs not yet met or satisfied. Why do people work? Apart from the obvious reasons of earning a salary, people work because it plays an important role in the development of self- respect and a sense of identity. A wide range of human needs is satisfied by working. The need for affiliation, feeling of competence and success, authority, control and pride are very key motivation for work. Knowing what your employees' needs are and putting in place strategies to motivate them on the basis of their needs is a major challenge for managers of each of the departments. That is why it is very important for managers to have a good knowledge of the various theories of motivation which can then be applied to the particular situations existing in one's environment of work. Stoner et. al. (1995:31- 2) posit that: "Theories are perspectives with which people make sense of their world experiences.". Theory involves a systematic grouping of interdependent concepts - that is mental images of anything formed by generalization from particulars. Principles are generalizations or hypotheses that have been tested for accuracy and appear to be true.

There are as many management theories as there are contributors to the subject. This is why some scholars have called this situation "the management theory jungle" (Koontz, 1961:174-188; 1962:24; 1980:175- 187).

Principles in management are fundamental truths, explaining relationships between two or more sets of variables, usually an independent variable and a dependent variable. Managers compare principles with realities on the ground; otherwise, they will be prescribing the wrong treatment for the ailment they are dealing with. The knowledge about theories will help managers to solve their day-to-day problems and forestall future ones that may occur in the organization. In sum, there are basically three main reasons why we have to study management theory.

First, theories provide a stable focus for understanding what we experience. A theory provides criteria for what is relevant. Second, theories enable us to communicate efficiently and thus move into more and more complex relationships with other people. Third, theories make it possible – indeed, challenge us – to keep learning about our world.

HUMAN BEHAVIOURAL AND MOTIVATIONAL THEORIES

Understanding why people behave the way they do is a major challenge to managers and leaders generally. Various researchers in the field of social sciences have come up with theories they believe will help organizational leaders to better relate with staff and help improve production. The various schools of management thought are materials or framework for the study of management. The schools of management thought are distinct and are based on different and, sometimes, contradictory assumptions about human beings and about the organizations for which they work.

During the present century, certain schools of management thought have developed. Each school reflects the problems of the period during which they were popular. Harold Koontz was the first who have attempted to classify the various approaches on management in the schools of management theory. Since the beginning of the study of management, several scholars, working in different eras or ages, have come up with what they believed to be important aspects of good management practice. Over time, management thinkers and researchers have sought ways to organize and classify the voluminous information about management that has been collected, collated and disseminated. These attempts at classification have resulted in the identification of what is referred to as management schools.

Disagreement exists as to the exact number of management schools. Different writers have identified as few as three and as many as twelve. The relatively large number of management schools of thought reflects a lack of consensus among management scholars about basic questions of theory and practice. For the purpose of this book, we shall discuss the following management schools of thought:

a. The Scientific Management School comprising the works of Frederick W. Taylor and Lillian Gilbreth's motion study, among others;
b. The Classical Organizational Theory School comprising Henri Fayol's views on administration, and Max Weber's idealized bureaucracy, among others;
c. The Behavioural School comprising the work of Elton Mayo and his associates;
d. The Management Science School and;
e. Recent Developments in Management Theory comprises, among others, the Team Building approach and the Learning Organizations.

Scientific Management School

The first management theory is what people popularly refer to as Frederick Taylor's Scientific Management. Frederick Winslow Taylor, in carrying out his studies, devised a system he called scientific management, a form of industrial engineering that established the organization of work using the Ford assembly line as a case study or basis. This discipline, along with the industrial psychology put in place by others who also worked at the Hawthorne Works of Western Electric in the 1920s, progressed management theory from early time- and-motion studies to the latest total quality control ideas. His works entail the following: 1. "Find the one 'best way' to perform each task. 2. Carefully match each worker to each task. 3. Closely supervise workers and use reward and punishment as motivators, and 4. The task of management is planning and control". While this theory proved successful in the simple industrialized companies at the turn of the century, it has not fared well in modern companies. The philosophy of 'production first, and people second' or simply put – 'produce or perish' has left the legacy of declining production and quality. Taylor' s ideas were greatly misinterpreted by those who applied them. As a result, staff unions condemned speedups and the lack of voice in work that 'Taylorism' gave to them. Quality of goods and services and productivity fell when his principles were applied hook-line-and sinker without modification.

The Classical Organization Theory

Henry Fayol developed fourteen principles of management and six functions of management. His work has been an influence on modern management theory, and the four basic functions of managers we discussed at the beginning of this book are part of his recommendations. Although the fourteen principles are not being used today, they can still offer guidance to modern day managers. Max Weber, a German sociologist, philosopher and political economist equally contributed to this school of thought.

Weber talked so much about the beauty of ideal bureaucracy. He believed that an ideal bureaucracy consists of six specific characteristics:

1) Specialization and Division of Labor; 2) Hierarchical Authority Structures; 3) Rules and Regulations; 4) Technical Competence Guidelines; 5) Impersonality and Personal Indifference; 6) A Standard of Formal, Written Communications. Although the perspective provided by the classical school of thought encourages efficiency, it is often criticized as ignoring human needs or people issues. Also, it rarely takes into consideration

human error or the variability of work performances (each worker is different).

Behavioural School

The key contributor under this category is Elton Mayo of the Harvard Business School and his associates who were invited to carry out some studies at the Hawthorne Works of Western Electric Company, Chicago. Their experiment demonstrated that the productivity of the employees is not the function of only the physical conditions of work and money wages paid to them. Productivity of employees depends heavily upon the satisfaction of the employees in their work situations. From my experience as a staff union leader, employee satisfaction is relative. What satisfies a particular staff may not necessarily satisfy another category of staff. For instance, staff at the junior level in the organization tend to settle for monetized remunerations like lump sum payments and salary increases while the ones at the senior and management levels want, in addition to their salaries, job security, together with long term incentives like health insurance, retirement benefits, allocation of shares, job description and the intangible privileges that follow.

The Management Science Approach

The management science approach, which is also known as quantitative approach came up from the early application of the scientific management techniques because of complexities of organizations. Today's managers are required to have more and better information in order to make effective decisions. A wide variety of quantitative tools have been developed and high-speed computers deployed in the analysis of information. One problem with this approach is that it requires the application of complicated equipment that requires special training to understand and use. While this approach has found wide applications in planning and control activities, not all managerial processes can be rationalized and quantified. Dealing with people most of the time require the use of the heart and not the head, otherwise the manager would be perceived to be anti-people in his approach.

RECENT DEVELOPMENTS IN MANAGEMENT THEORY

Since the development in the field of management theory continues, there have been recent developments which seek to improve the way we understand ourselves and how we can get more from each other without the old bottlenecks and resistance witnessed in the past. Under this category of theory are the Systems Approach, Situational or Contingency Theory, Chaos Theory and Team Building Theory.

Team Building

Many large multinational organizations, especially those who want to maintain their industry position, and retain and even improve their market share are rushing their staff through team building classes. It has come to the notice of modern management that the problem of low productivity and decrease in staff morale comes from the failure of management to build trust between employers and employees. People help build what they help suggest. Once the employee comes to trust the employer, he or she owns the organizational vision as a personal vision and takes extra-ordinary steps to meet set goals and objectives.

The Learning Organization

Many large organizations today refer to themselves as 'learning organizations.' Learning was defined by Peter Senge (1990: 3) as "enhancing one's capacity to take action." Therefore, learning organizations are organizations that are continually improving their capacity to create value. Senge believes that organizations are moving and growing from bullying and controlling to predominantly learning and applying knowledge. Senge, under this research, discusses what he termed 'learning disabilities' in companies. He presented the disabilities to occur when people form a strong identification with their position. What they do becomes a function of their position. They see themselves in specific roles, and are unable to view their jobs as part of a larger system. This often leads to animosity towards others in the organization especially when things begin to go wrong. Another disability he saw is when we are slow to recognize gradual changes or threats. According to Senge, there are five disciplines important to the learning organization. The first discipline is 'building a shared vision.' The second is 'personal mastery' which demonstrates a commitment to the vision of the organization. The third discipline involves 'the idea of mental models; where we construct internal representations of reality.' The fourth discipline is that only shared mental models are important to organizational learning. The fifth discipline is a commitment to a systems approach.

Learning organizations replace department heads with team leaders. The team leader understands the value in working as a team in favour of a know-it-all boss calling the shots from the top without ever allowing the subordinates to give their suggestions about how the organization can perform better or how certain tasks can be done better. It releases departments or units within the organization from the boxes where they hitherto operated and from where they throw stones sometimes at other units in the same company which they may ignorantly consider as adversaries or rivals. Leaning organizations emphasize the need to work with others because 'together we do it better; divided we fall, but together we stand'. They strive to remove administrative bottlenecks and bureaucracies that often slow down the decision-making process. They send their staff to team building events and teach them how to change from the old way of work to a new one. They aim to change staff attitudes in order to take the organization to a higher altitude. They manage issues before they grow big and become a threat, and they are environmentally friendly. They equally pay attention to and properly manage diversity issues within and without their organizations. Learning organizations are ahead of others that are rigid, conservative and closed in every area;

and they control a larger market share and are industry leaders in every field. Clearly that is the direction to go.

There are so many books on leadership out there that one may think there's hardly any need to write any more books on the subject. This book is specially written as my contribution to so many other books already written on the subject; with special focus on how to train and develop leaders for the future. This book is equally useful to both students studying Organizational Leadership in colleges as well as leaders in various fields of human endeavor who might find in it a useful addition to what they already know and practice about leadership.

BIBLIOGRAPHY

Addleson, M. (c 1998). What is a learning organization? Online. Available.

Akintomide, Y. (2005). Agagu urges NDDC to consult stakeholders on projects.

Amanda Credaro, (2006): Innovation and Change in Business: Warrior Librarian.

An Industry Perspective: Can Europe Resume the Catching Up Process? Luxembourg: European Commission.

Ash, Ket al (2001). Organizational Change and Development. Essex: Pearson Education Limited. Badham, R and Buchanan, D (2000) Power, Politics and Organizational Change. London: Sage Publications

B. Griggs & L. L. Louw (Eds.), Valuing Diversity: New Tools for a New Reality. McGraw Hill, Inc: New York.

Barack Obama (2006): Audacity of Hope. Penguine Books.

Bennett, S. (1998) Learning, change and organizations. Online. Available.

Brain Tracy, (1993): Maximum Achievement (The proven system and skills that will unluck your hidden powers to succeed): Beulahland publications, p6.

Burnes, B. (2000). Managing Change; A Strategic Approach to Organizational Dynamics. Essex: Pearson Education Limited

Carlopio, J. R. (1998). Implementation: Making Workplace Innovation and Technical Change Happen. Roseville, NSW: McGraw-Hill.

Carnall, A. C. (2003). Managing Change in Organizations. Essex: Pearson Education Limited.

Charles Fishman, (2006): The Wal-Mart Effect. Penguin books.

Chinua Achebe (1983): An Image of Africa and the Problem with Nigeria. Penguin Books

Christopher Matthews, (2012): Wal-Mart at 50 Years: How Retail Giant Changed the World, Time.com.

Clyde, L. (1983). Australian school libraries in the nineteenth century. Australian Library Journal 32 (2), pp 11 -17.

Dunning, C. (1997). Got change for a paradigm? From Gutenberg to hypertext. Online. Available. Updated April 15, 1997.

E. Burton Swanson (1997): The Organizing Vision in Information System Innovation. p. 458-474.

Eisenhardt, K. (1989) 'Making fast strategic decisions in high-velocity environments', *Academy of Management Journal,* 32 (3), 543-576,

Ensley, M., Pearce, C., and Hmieleski, K. (2006) 'The moderating effect of environmental dynamism on the relationship between entrepreneur leadership behavior and new venture performance', *Journal of Business Venturing,* 21.

Freeman, A. (1999). Organization of resources. Introductory Talk for Charles Sturt Subject ETL403. Macquarie University, February 12, 1999.

Fullan, M.G. (1993). The school as a learning organization. In Changing forces: Probing the depths of educational reform. London: Falmer Press. 42 - 83.

Fullan, M.G. et al (1990). Linking classroom and school improvement. Educational Leadership May 1990, 13-19.

Griggs, L. B. (1995). Valuing Diversity: Where From… Where To? In L. B. Griggs & L. L. Louw (Eds.), Valuing diversity: New tools for a new reality (pp. 1- 14).

Griggs, L. B. (1995). Valuing Relationship: The Heart of Valuing Diversity. In L. B. Griggs & L. L. Louw (Eds.).

Hargreaves, A. (1993). Collaboration: A key to leadership for quality in education. The Practicing Administrator, 15 (3), 16 - 18.

Hersey, P. (1985). The Situational Leader. New York, NY: Warner Books.

Hersey, P. and Blanchard, K.H. (1977). Management

Hill, J. (1995). Teacher librarians: Leaders and learners in the school learning community. Scan, 14 (3), 47 - 49.

Knowledge. London: SAGE, pp. 141-54.

Kurt Lewin: (1951): Change Management Model. Academy of Management Journal, *37(5):* 1141-66.

Lashway, L. (1998). Creating a learning organization. ERIC Database. Online.

Lee, G (2003) Leadership Coaching. London: Chartered Institute of Personnel Development.

Limerick, D. and Cunnington, B. (1993). Managing the new organization: A blueprint for networks and strategic alliances. Sydney: Business and Professional Publications.

Limerick, D. et al (1994). Transformational change. The Learning Organization. Online.

Lincoln, P. (1987). A view from the inside. In The Learning School . Boston Spa: The British Library. 6 - 28.

Lohor, J., and P. Ohia (2004). Nigeria 3rd Most Corrupt Country - Tl. http://www.thisdayonline.com/news/20041021news04.html

Mabey, C and Mayon - White, B, ed. (1993). Managing Change. London: Paul Chapman Publishing Limited.

Mole, K. F. & Mender Ram (2012): Perspectives in Entrepreneurship: A critical Approach. *Basingstoke* John C. Maxwell (2003): *Thinking for* a *Change.* Warner *Business* Books, 2003, ISBN

Newman, J. (1998). We can't get there from here. Critical Issues in School Reform. Phi Delta Kappa International. Online.

Nonaka, I. (1988). Creating organizational order out of chaos: Self-renewal in Japanese firms. California Management Review, 30 (3), 57 - 73.

O'Connor, C. (1993). The Handbook for Organizational Change. Maidenhead: McGraw-Hill Ogbonna, J (2005) Towards a Pragmatic Reform Agenda. http://allafrica.com/stories/printable/200509200150.html

O'Donnell, D., Mcguire, D. and Cross, C. (2006) "Critically challenging some assumptions in HRD," *International Journal of Training and Development,* 10(1): 4-16.

O'Dwyer, M. and Ryan, E. (2000) "Management development issues for owners/managers of micro-enterprises" *Journal of European Industrial Training,* 24(6): 345-50.

OECD (2003) *Management Training in SMEs: Synthesis Report.* Paris: Organization for Economic Cooperation and Development.

Ogbonna, E. and Harris, L. (1998) Managing organizational culture: compliance or genuine change? *British Journal of Management,* 9: 273-88.

Olsson, S. (2002) Gendered heroes: male and female self-representations of executive identity. *Women in Management Review,* 17(3/4): 142-50.

O'Mahoney, M. and de Boer, W. (2002) Britain's Relative Productivity Performance: Updates from 1999. London: National Institute of Economic and Social Research.

O'Mahoney, M. and Van Ark, B. (eds.) (2004) *EU Productivity and Competitiveness:*

Ortenblad, A. (2002) Organizational learning: a radical perspective. *International Journal of Management Reviews,* 4(1): 87-100.

Ostroff, C., Atwater, L. and Feinberg, B. (2004) Understanding self-other agreement: a look at rater and rate characteristics, context and outcomes. *Personnel Psychology,* 57: 333-75.

Osuji, T.O (2005). Public Opinion And Public Policy In Nigeria. http://nigeriavillagesquare.com/index2.php?option=comcontent&task=view&i

Oswick, C. and Grant, D. (1996) *Organization Development: Metaphorical Explorations.* London: Pitman.

Oswick, C., Anthony, P., Keenoy, T., Mangham, I. and Grant, D. (2000) A dialogic analysis of organizational learning. *Journal of Management Studies,* 376(6): 887-902.

Paauwe, J. and Williams, R. (2001) Seven key issues for management development. *Journal of Management Development,* 20(2): 90-102.

Palmer, I. and Dunford, R. (1996) Interrogating reframing: evaluating metaphor-based analysis of organizations. In S. Clegg and G. Palmer (eds), *The Politics of Management*

Parker, M. (1999) Capitalism, subjectivity and ethics: debating labour process analysis. *Organization Studies,* 20(1): 25-45.

Parker, M. (2000) 'The less important sideshow': the limits of epistemology in organizational analysis. *Organization,* 7(3): 519-23.

Parker, M. (2002a) *Against Management.* Cambridge: Polity Press.

Parker, M. (2002b) Queering management and organization. Gen der, *Work and Organization,* 9(2): 147-66.

Paton, R., Taylor, S. and Storey, J. (2004) Corporate universities and leadership development. In J. Storey (ed.), *Leadership in Organizations.* London: Routledge, pp. 81-102.

Pattison, S. (1997) *The Faith of the Managers: When Management Becomes Religion.* London: Cassell.

Patton, D. and Marlow, S. (2002) The determinants of management training within smaller firms in the UK: what role does strategy play? *Journal of Small Business and Enterprise Development,* 9(3): 260-70.

Reigeluth Charles, (1994): Educational Learning Theories. World Meteorological Organization (WMC) (2010: The Global Climate between 2001-2010

Rifkin, J. (1995). The end of work: The decline of the global labor force and the dawn of the post market era. New York: G.P. Putnam's Sons.

Rogers, M. E (2003). Diffusion of Innovations. New York: Free Press.

Santos, A. (c 1999). Characteristics of the learning Organization. Online.

Schuyler, G. (1997). A paradigm shift from instruction to learning. ERIC Digest. ED 41496.

Senge, P. et al (1994). The fifth discipline: Strategies and tools for building a learning organization. New York: Doubleday.

Shields, P. (1989). Concerns-based adoption model. In D. Driscoll (ed.) Implementing change: A cooperative approach. Vancouver, BC: British Columbia Teacher-Librarians' Association. pp 36 - 61.

Sultan Rehman Sherief (2004): African Economic Analysis PDF The Fly Fisherman Guide to the Meaning of Life.

Tinkler, D. (1996). Information literacy - the effect of new technology on literacy. Ockham's Razor. ABC Radio National Transcript, Sunday 29th, September, 1996. Online. Available.

Whitely, A. (1995). The core values model. In Managing change: A core values approach. Melbourne: Macmillan Education. pp 42 - 65.

Wind, J. Y., & Main, J. (1998). Driving Change. New York: Free Press.

Yee, J.A. (1998). Forces motivating institutional reform. ERIC Digest. ED 421179. Online.

www.ingramcontent.com/pod-product-compliance
Ingram Content Group UK Ltd.
Pitfield, Milton Keynes, MK11 3LW, UK
UKHW022022190726
13853UKWH00005B/2054

9 789789 912377